SCRIPTURE BAPTISM

DEFENDED,

AND

ANABAPTIST NOTIONS

PROVED TO BE

ANTI-SCRIPTURAL NOVELTIES.

BY

REV. JOHN LEVINGTON.

"Then remembered I the word of the Lord, how that he said, John indeed baptized with water; but ye shall be baptized with the Holy Ghost."—Acts xi. 16.

"Suffer the little children to come unto me, and forbid them not: for of such is the Kingdom of God."—Mark x. 14.

"Therefore, as by the offence of one judgment came upon all men to condemnation, even so by the righteousness of one the free gift came upon all men unto justification of life.—Rom. v. 18.

"Where sin abounded grace did much more abound."—Rom. v. 20.

SOLD BY T. K. ADAMS, DETROIT.
ALSO,
AT THE METHODIST BOOK DEPOSITORY; AND BY THE AUTHOR, MONROE, MICH.
AND BY BOOKSELLERS GENERALLY.

1865

Rev. Dr. Duffield
with the Christian regards
of the Author
Sept. 1, 1865. John Levington

CONTENTS.

CHAPTER I.

CHAPTER II.

CHAPTER III.

CHAPTER X.

CHAPTER XI.

CHAPTER XII.

CHAPTER XIII.

CHAPTER XIV.

CHAPTER XV.

INTRODUCTORY REMARKS.

During the past winter, the M. E. Church in this city held a protracted meeting, and it pleased God to give efficiency to his word, and to bless the labors of his people and crown them with much success. The Presbyterians also held a protracted meeting at the same time, and although each Church attended to its own work, there was a free intercourse of both pastors and members; each attending the meetings of their sister Church when an opportunity offered.

Thus things went on pleasantly and prosperously till the Anabaptists commenced to work in their usual way, preaching and urging their peculiar views, publicly, and from house to house. Their baptism was the only baptism; "there was no other mode practised for more than fifteen hundred years." Baptism was "neither more nor less than to dip, plunge, dive, or immerse under the pressure of the minister's hand." And as their baptism was the only baptism, their Church, of course, was the only

Church. It was loudly demanded, "Where was the Methodist Church before John Wesley? Where was the Presbyterian Church before John Calvin?" Our economy was attacked and our "Class-book" pronounced "a mere catchtrap." The members of my charge were visited in their own houses, and the Bible taken from the shelf to prove that our baptism was no baptism, and that plunging only was baptism; then they were kindly assured that the baptist door was open, and that if they would come they would be accepted and receive scripture baptism.

Thus the work of proselyting was pushed forward with a zeal and a perseverance worthy of a better cause. And those poor dupes who were caught in this way were made to renounce their baptism, brought to the river, and made "to plunge, dip, dive, or immerse, under pressure of the minister's hand."

Now they became exceeding bold, and even boasted of their success in proselyting, so much so that a certain lady very boastfully said to one of our people, "We will have three or four more of your Methodist ladies." But though matters were arranged in full confidence of leading them and several others to the river, they were deprived of that pleasure; a little instruction under the blessing of God saved them from that snare! A young lady, I think one of the expected four, and a young convert, afterward told me that "Mr. H. followed her till she was almost distracted and so distressed that she wept. And when she told him that she thought our baptism was proper baptism, he threateningly said, "How dare you say so?" She says she actually trembled. She having been converted in our meetings and received into our Church some time before, I said, "Why did you not come and tell me?" She said, "I was so perplexed I did not know what to do." I think these were her words.

Some young men who, like many others, became filled with these ideas, and seemed to think that they were now prepared to prove anything and everything, came into my Bible Class and desired me to bring up the subject of baptism there; but I told them, "No, it is my custom when others are at it to let them blow off, and then I will attend to it." Efforts were also made to unsettle the minds of our Sabbath School children, and means employed to that end similar to those already mentioned; nor were they employed without effect. Teachers came to me telling me that I must do something, for many of the children had become very uneasy; one whole class I was requested to talk to, and did so, and succeeded, I think, in restoring their quiet.

But time would fail to tell all, and some is really too bad to be told; and I have concluded not to tell it. Suffice it to say, that my pastoral abilities were heavily taxed; but by diligence and the blessing of God I succeeded in saving most of the sheep; though I am well convinced that much harm was done by the doings of these proselyters; and I have had much sorrow and have wept many tears in consequence. For while we labored simply to lead sinners to Jesus for salvation, they labored to bring them to the river for immersion; while we labored to convert them to God, they labored to convert them to their peculiar notions!

Finally, I called the Church together, having previously called the attention of the official board to the matter, and having also conversed previously with some of the leading brethren alone. I stated some of the facts to the Church, saying as now, that there were other things that I would forbear to tell, at least for the present. Some of the older brethren, and others, expressed their disapprobation of such doings and gave wise counsel. I also gave what I conceived to be good advice; others told their experience, and appropriately referred to what they had witnessed in days of Millerite and Campbellite excitement, and prophesied that these efforts would come to naught, as those did. And having thus talked, and sung, and prayed, we departed, trusting in the Lord.

Finally, on Sunday, the 23d of April, I announced that I would preach on baptism on the following Sunday, which I did twice, and so I did on each of the two following Sabbaths, six sermons in all; and from that time till now none have been made "to plunge, dip, or dive, under the pressure of the minister's hand!" In the following pages you have the substance of these sermons, for most of what I said was written before delivery. I thought it necessary to state these facts, that the reader might appreciate some of the remarks in the following pages. Moreover, this is not the first time that I have been annoyed in this way.

In referring to the denomination with whose teachings I join issue, it was necessary, of course, to use some distinctive appellation. I did not think it proper to use the appellation Baptist, for that term is calculated and designed to convey the idea that the denomination to which it is applied is the only denomination that baptizes at all. But so far is this from being true that it would be more in harmony with truth to call them Antibaptists, seeing they are opposed to the baptism of children, that is, to the baptism of the whole human race till a given period is reached. I have, therefore, used the appellation Anabaptists, as they were originally and properly called, because they rebaptized. I have also used the appellation Antipedobaptists, because they are opposed to the baptism of children. And, for the sake of convenience, I have sometimes used the appellation Immersionists, though, strictly speaking, that is not correct, for they do not immerse, as we have shown, but they plunge, and plunge only; but we did not like to use the appellation *plungers*, though it would be a truthful appellation, but it has a strange want of euphony about it.

If any person, after carefully reading this little work, will honestly say to me, "I still believe that the views objected to are the right views," I here promise that I will return to such the price of the pamphlet and take it back cheerfully.

I think this work is needed, for everything of importance and relevant to the subject is pressed into this small compass, and so stated, I think, that everybody may read and understand. For the same purpose I have caused the Greek quotations to be printed in English characters.

JOHN LEVINGTON.

MONROE, MICHIGAN.

CHRISTIAN BAPTISM—THE MODE.

CHAPTER I.

Position of Anabaptists Stated—The words Dip, Plunge, Immerse, Overwhelm, not Synonymous—They give us the word Plunge as the Synonym of Baptize, and their practice is to Plunge, and Plunge only—Their favorite arguments drawn from the Baptism by John and that by Philip—John's Baptism not Christian Baptism—Christ's Baptism different from both—Their Arguments based upon a mere Assumption—Their Assumption is shown to involve palpable Absurdities—It is disproved and shown to be a mere begging of the question.

The position of the Anabaptists with regard to the *mode* of baptism, is this. They say, "Baptism is neither more nor less than an immersion of the whole body in water, solemnly performed in the name of the Father, and of the Son, and of the Holy Ghost." Their arguments in favor of this position are usually commenced thus, by their writers: "Baptism, from the Greek word *Baptizo*, or *Bapto*, *I dip or plunge.*" "To dip, plunge or immerse." They also use the word *overwhelm*, and sometimes other words which they consider synonymous with these. *Baptize*, *dip*, *plunge*, *immerse*, *overwhelm.* It is assumed that these five terms are synonymous, but we deny that any one of them is synonymous with any other one of the five terms. It is not necessary, however, to refute this unwarrantable assumption, seeing it is *plunging* and *plunging only*, that is practised by those with whom we join issue, nor do I know any other word in the English language that expresses their practice quite as well as this one does; *submerge* is the next best. Be this as it may, however, their practice is to *plunge under water*, and this and this *only*, they assert, is baptism; and they say the Greek word *baptizo* means this, "neither more nor less." It is necessary that this should be distinctly noticed, as Baptists, so-called, seem to prefer the word *immerse*, though it is a somewhat ambiguous word, and does not fairly express their practice. Inasmuch, then, as this word is that which best expresses their practice, and as they claim it to be the *synonym* of baptize, we will use it in these discussions, as appropriately expressing that for which they contend, and to which we object.

The most favorite arguments of the Anabaptists in favor of plunging are drawn from the record of the baptism by John, and from the record of the baptism by Philip, *and are all based upon the assumption, that certain words have the meaning which they attach to them, and no other.* Now we purpose to prove that the reverse of this assumption is true, and will thus take away the very foundation of their arguments, and render them worthless.

As John's baptism is so much relied upon by the Anabaptists, it may be well, just here to call attention to the fact that, his baptism was not Christian Baptism, and, consequently, cannot properly be claimed as a pattern for Christians to go by. The following remarks will suffice to show that John's baptism was not Christian baptism. 1. John's baptism was "unto repentance," and the parties baptized professed faith in a Saviour *to come.* 2. Christian baptism is the *initiatory right into the Christian Church;* but when John Baptized, the Christian Church had no existence. 3. While John's baptism was "unto repentance," Christian baptism is the seal of justification already received, as circumcision was. Hence when those who had been baptized by John, believed, and were justified in the Christian sense, the Apostles administered Christian baptism to them, as we learn from the following Scripture; "Paul having passed through the upper coasts, came to Ephesus; and finding certain disciples, he said unto them, Have ye received the Holy Ghost since ye believed? And they said unto him, We have not so much as heard whether there be any Holy Ghost. And he said unto them, Unto what then were ye baptized? And they said, Unto John's baptism. Then said Paul, John verily baptized with the baptism of repentance, saying unto the people, that they should believe on him which should come after him, that is, on Christ Jesus. When they heard this, they were baptized in the name of the Lord Jesus. Acts xix. 1-5. See also Matt. iii. 5. It is entirely unnecessary to say any more to prove that John's baptism was not Christian baptism. And as the baptism of our blessed Lord is constantly referred to by the Anabaptists, who tell us that we must follow Jesus, it may be well to remark that neither was that Christian baptism, nor was it the same as that which John administered to his countrymen; it could not be unto repentance, for Jesus had no sin to repent of, neither could it be the seal of his justification, for he never was pardoned; nor was it the right of initiation into the Christian Church, for the Christian Church did not yet exist; but like the Jewish high-priest, he was thus initiated into the priests' office; it was also the sign of the baptism by the Holy Ghost, and that was administered by the Spirit "descending upon him." Thus we might fairly reject all the arguments drawn from John's baptism without saying any more. We will not, however, rest our cause here, but will now proceed to refute their assumption, viz., that the words *baptizo*, *en*, *eis*, and *ek* have the meaning which they say they have, and no other.

We now take up the word *baptizo;* and here let it be distinctly noticed that the advocates of *plunging* as the *only* mode of baptism, give us the word *plunge* as the *synonym* of the word *baptize*, and their practice is *plunging*, and *only plunging;* nor will they admit that anything short of this is *baptism*. We have nothing to do, then, with the words, *dip*, *immerse*, *overwhelm*, or any other; their use only tends to deceive*;* *baptizo* we are told means to *plunge the whole body under*, and their practice corresponds with the assertion; they do not *dip*, they do not *immerse*, they *plunge only!*

The question, then, is simply this: does *baptizo* mean to *plunge*, "neither more nor less?" To refute this assumption we have only to quote a few texts where the word occurs, and substitute the word *plunge* for the word *baptize*.

Luke xvi, 24. "Send Lazarus that he may *plunge* the tip of his finger in water and cool my tongue." John xii. 20. "He to whom I shall give a sop when I have *plunged* it." Rev. xix. 13, he was clothed in a vesture *plunged* in blood." Matt. xxvi. 23. He that *plungeth* his hand with Me in the dish, the same shall betray me." Mark xiv. 20. "One of the twelve that *plungeth* with me in the dish." John xiii. 26. "He it is to whom I shall give a sop when I have *plunged* it." Mark vii. 4, 8. "And when they come from market, except they *plunge* they eat not. And many other things there be, which they have received to hold, as the *plunging* of cups, and pots, and brazen vessels, and tables." The word *klinon*, here translated tables, means, more properly, couches, or beds; more especially those couches or lounges upon which the Jews reclined at their tables; these were, say, fourteen feet long, more or less. Now what do you think of plunging these lounges, or tables, under water before eating? The idea is so absurd that the mere mention of it is sufficient. But this is only one of the numerous absurdities implied in the assumption to which we object. It will be remembered, of course, that *baptismos* in this passage, is rendered *washing*, by our translators, but the assumption to which we object will have it *plunging!* But we proceed. Heb. ix. 10. "Divers *plungings*, and carnal ordinances, imposed on them until the time of reformation." Heb. vi. 2. "Of the doctrine of *plungings*, and of laying on of hands, and of resurrection of the dead, and of eternal judgment." What think you of the doctrine of *plungings?* Matt. iii. 11. "Indeed *plunge* you with water unto repentance; but he that cometh after me is mightier than I, whose shoes I am not worthy to bear. He shall *plunge* you with the Holy Ghost and with fire." If the advocates of plunging insist on the substitution of *in* for *with*, then the reading will be "He shall *plunge* you *in* the Holy Ghost and in fire!" If they prefer this rendering they are welcome to it! But we think men of sober judgment will not hesitate to pronounce both renderings absurd, and intolerable. Yet this must be the rendering or the assumption which we object must be given up. "Then cometh Jesus from Galilee to Jordan unto John, to be *plunged* of him. But John forbade him, saying, I have need to be *plunged* of thee, and comest thou to me?" Acts. xi. 16. "Then remembered I the word of the Lord, how that he said John indeed *plunged* in water; but ye shall be *plunged* in the Holy Ghost." Nothing prevents such language from being blasphemy but the good intention of those who use it. In Matt. xx. 22, 23 it is difficult to get the word *plunge* in at all; but if we substitute the word *plunge* for the word baptize, these verses will read thus: "Are ye able to be *plunged* with the *plunging* that I am *plunged* with?" "Ye shall drink indeed of my cup, and be *plunged* with the *plunging* that I am *plunged* with." Mark i. 4. "John did *plunge* in the wilderness, and preach the *plunging* of repentance for the remission of sins." John xii. 50. "But I have a *plunging* to be *plunged* with; and how am I straitened till it be accomplished." Acts x. 37. "That word, I say, ye know, which was published throughout all Judea, and began from Galilee, after the *plunging* which John preached." Acts xiii. 24. "John preached the *plunging* of repentance to all the people of Israel." In Acts xix. 3, we read, "And he said unto them, Unto what then were ye baptized? And they said, Unto John's baptism." The word here rendered *unto*, is, in the original, *eis*, and the advocates of plunging rest their arguments, as we shall show by-and-by, upon the assumption that *eis* always means ***into***; now let us substitute *into* for *unto*, in this verse, and *plunge* for *baptize*, as they claim we should, and the passage will read thus: "And he said unto them, *into* what then were ye *plunged?* And they said, *into* John's *plunging!*" Now who but an ignorant fanatic would charge the inspired writers with talking such consummate nonsense as this transaction indicates? And, remember this is the correct translation if the assumption here opposed be true; and it is to obtain such a translation as this that the Anabaptists have got up their new Bible! 1 Cor. xii. 13. "For by one Spirit are we all *plunged* into one body." Once more, according to this assumption, Rom. vi. 3 and 4 will read thus: "Know ye not that so many of us as were *plunged into* Jesus Christ, were *plunged into* his death? Therefore we are buried with him by *plunging into* death."

We think we have now given plunging enough to satisfy the most ardent lover of plunging; nay, we think enough has been given to make the most ardent lover of plunging sick of it! We beg to assure the reader, however, that much more of the same kind might be given; what is here given is a mere tithe of the absurdities involved in the *assumption* that *baptizo* always means to *plunge*, "neither more nor less!" We are aware that the better informed among the Anabaptists admit that *baptizo* has other meaning; but, notwithstanding this, their *arguments* are based upon the *assumption* that *this is its only meaning;* and they give us the word *plunge* as its *synonym;* and they practice *plunging* and *plunging only!* Moreover, we deny that either the word *dip* or the word *immerse*, properly expresses their practice, nor does *overwhelm*, for you may overwhelm a man by casting abundance of water, sand, or other substance upon him, but that is not plunging, and, consequently, not baptism, if the assumption under consideration be correct; and if it is not correct, not true, as it evidently is not, all the arguments which assume its truthfulness, and depend upon such assumption for their validity and conclusiveness, are worthless; till the point assumed is proved, all such arguments are *a mere begging of the question.* In conclusion, we beg to remind the reader that the word PLUNGE, in its different forms, in the above remarks, represents the word *baptizo*, in its corresponding forms in the original; and if the substitution of the one word for the other involves us in absurdities, and even implies impossibilities, as it evidently does, then to baptize does not mean to plunge, and the assumption that it does is not true, and all the arguments built upon that assumption, are worthless, are a mere begging of the question. This is what we claim to have proved, and this is what we undertook to prove, in this chapter.

CHAPTER II.

Direct Argument taken up—That which God calls Baptism shown to be administered by the baptismal element Falling upon the Subject—This is claimed to be a Fact—What God Asserts Baptists Deny—God Baptizes by Pouring—This, too, is a Fact—His Precept and his Practice Against Plunging.

WE will now proceed to the direct evidence in the case, and will show that *what God calls baptism is administered by the baptismal element falling upon the party baptized, not by the party being plunged in that element;* and will, consequently, prove that the mode contended for and practised by the Anabaptists, is just the reverse of God's mode.

In Daniel iv. 33, we read: "The same hour was the thing fulfilled upon Nebuchadnezzar: and he was driven from men, and did eat grass as oxen, and his body was wet [*ebaphē*] with the dew of heaven." Now, here is no plunging; yet Nebuchadnezzar was baptized. How was he baptized? The sacred writer tells you in these words: "his body was baptized with the dew of heaven." Now, everybody knows that "the dew of heaven" fell upon his body, and God calls this baptism. Nor can the Anabaptists force *en*, or *eis*, into their service in this case, for neither of these prepositions is found here; the record is, that "his body was baptized *with* the dew of heaven." See Septuagint, Chap. iv. 30. It is worthy of remark, too, that the descent and influences of the Spirit upon the human soul are compared to the descent and influences of the rain, and of the dew upon vegetation; hence we read thus in Ps. lxxii. 6: "He shall come down like rain upon the mown grass; as showers that water the earth." And in Hosea iv. 5, we read: "I will be as the dew unto Israel, he shall grow as the lily, and cast forth his roots as Lebanon." This is what God calls the baptism with the Spirit, and the falling of the dew upon Nebuchadnezzar is baptism with dew, or water. Yet this is what the advocates of plunging *despise, treat with contempt, and pronounce no baptism.* It is enough for us, however, to know that *God calls it baptism;* and that he calls it baptism *is a fact, an indisputable fact;* for we give his words, and the chapter and verse where they may be found. And, while the descent of the Spirit is compared to the descent of water in the form of rain or dew, we aver that it never is, and cannot be, compared to plunging the body into the water, nor is it ever compared to a dash of water overwhelming the body: such figures are of human invention, and, like all other errors, flow from the carnal nature, which always seeks for a great display, and loses the Spirit in the letter! To such Jesus still has to say: "The flesh profiteth nothing, the words that I speak unto you, they are spirit and they are life." And to such Paul says: "Are ye not yet carnal and walk as men?" We will now produce another text to prove that what God calls baptism was administered by the baptismal element falling upon the parties baptized. In 1 Cor. x. 1, 2, Paul says: "All our fathers were under the cloud, and all passed through the sea; and were all baptized unto Moses in the cloud and in the sea." Paul says, "all passed through the sea;" and Moses says, "The children of Israel walked upon dry land in the midst of the sea." Now, here was no plunging; the people were "under the cloud," and "upon dry land in the midst of the sea;" consequently the water with which they were baptized must have fallen upon them, whether it came from the cloud, which was suspended over them, or from the sea, which was "a wall unto them on their right hand and on their left." Here, again, was no plunging; the Israelites were not plunged in the cloud, for that was *over* them; nor in the sea, for the waters were "a wall," on either hand, while they "walked upon dry land." Their number was six hundred thousand men, beside women and children. To talk about plunging all these either in the cloud or in the sea is preposterous, yet they were all *baptized*, and they were baptized by *sprinkling*, and this sprinkling God calls baptism. This, too, is *a fact, an indisputable fact!* Neither were the Egyptians *plunged*, they were *overwhelmed with a vengeance;* but, observe, God does not call the *overwhelming* of the Egyptians baptism, but the sprinkling of the Israelites he does! Yet Anabaptists treat sprinkling with sovereign contempt, and are wont to say of those who were baptized by sprinkling, "They were sprinkled, *not baptized.*" In a word, that which God calls baptism they say is no baptism; what God affirms, they deny; these are the facts in the case!

Having shown that sprinkling, or pouring, is baptism, *that God says it is*, we now declare that we do not find a single text in God's book where that mode of baptism practised by the Anabaptists is enjoined, nor do I remember a single text wherein plunging is called baptism; if there is, let the advocates of plunging produce it; but, remember, if they should produce fifty such texts, it will not affect our argument, for still the fact claimed remains the same, viz: that, sprinkling, or pouring, is baptism—*God says it is.* Nor does God ever *plunge* when he baptizes, He always baptizes by *pouring*, *sprinkling*, *shedding*, falling, as we shall now show.

The baptism of the Spirit, and more especially that peculiar baptism which belongs to the times of the Gospel, is thus spoken of and promised by the prophets. Isaiah xliv. 3: "For I will pour water upon him that is thirsty, and floods upon the dry ground: I will pour my Spirit upon thy seed, and my blessing upon thine offspring." Here the sign, *water*, and the thing signified, the *Spirit*, are both spoken of, and the administration of each is said to be by *pouring:* "I will *pour* water," "I will *pour* my Spirit." It is quite evident that the pouring of water mentioned in this text represents the outpouring of the Spirit—the prophet, or rather the Lord, explains the one by the other. The same *baptism* is spoken of in the following prophetic promise: "And it shall come to pass afterward, that I will *pour out* my Spirit upon all flesh; and your sons and your daughters shall prophesy, your old men shall dream dreams, your young men shall see visions; and also upon the servants and upon the handmaids in those days will I *pour out* my Spirit."

In these and similar scriptures we have what our Lord calls "*The promise of the Father*," and what he and his apostles call the baptism of the Spirit. I do not know that this statement will be questioned as to its correctness, but if it should, the following texts will put it beyond question. Luke xxiv. 49: "And behold I send the promise of my Father upon you: but tarry ye in the city of Jerusalem until ye be endued with power from on high." Acts i. 4, 5: "He commanded them that they should not depart from Jerusalem, but wait for the promise of the Father, which, saith he, ye have heard of me. For John truly baptized with water, but ye shall be baptized with the Holy Ghost not many days hence." In these prophetic promises there are two particulars to which, more especially, we call attention. First, the thing promised, *baptism:* "Ye shall be baptized with the Holy Ghost." Second, that baptism was to be administered by *pouring:* "I will pour out my Spirit;" and the same is said of the outward and visible sign of this baptism, the baptism with water: "I will pour water upon him that is thirsty." It is evident, according to these prophetic promises, that baptism, in every sense of the word, was to be by *pouring.* This, too, we claim to be a fact!

Let us now turn to the New Testament and see how these prophetic promises were fulfilled. Acts ii. 1–4: "And when the day of Pentecost was fully come, they were all with one accord in one place; And suddenly there came a sound from heaven, as of a rushing mighty wind, and it filled all the house where they were sitting. And there appeared unto them cloven tongues like as of fire, and it sat upon each of them. And they were all filled with the Holy Ghost." Observe, the parties baptized on this occasion were all in one room and remained unmoved till baptized—there was no plunging. Second, The sound "filled all the house where they were sitting;" observe, they were sitting when baptized.

2

Third, the Holy Ghost filled the parties baptized; and, fourth, the symbol sat upon each of them; and, finally, all came from above. Now, this is what God calls baptism; and it was administered by *pouring*, by *falling*, as both the prophets and Jesus Christ said it would be. There was no plunging!

Now, when Peter witnessed all this he "Lifted up his voice and said unto them: Ye men of Judea, and all ye that dwell at Jerusalem, be this known unto you, and hearken to my words:" "This is that which was spoken by the prophet Joel, And it shall come to pass in the last days, saith God, I will pour out my Spirit upon all flesh;" "And on my servants, and on my handmaidens, I will pour out, in those days, of my Spirit." Here the apostle Peter declares that the prophetic promise, quoted above, the promise of the Father, was fulfilled by this pentecostal baptism of the Spirit; and this baptism was by *pouring*, as the foregoing prophecy said it would be.

Here let it be remembered that the Anabaptists assert, that *baptizo* means to *plunge*, and that it means "neither more nor less;" hence they practice plunging, and plunging only, and assert that *pouring*, *sprinkling*, is no baptism! But it is an indispensable fact that the Spirit was *poured out and fell upon the disciples, upon the day of Pentecost, while they were* SITTING! And it is a fact equally indisputable, that Jesus Christ and his apostles, and the whole Christian Church from then till now, call this baptism! Here, then, is baptism without plunging; here is baptism by *pouring;* let Anabaptists pronounce it no baptism if they dare! If they do, they contradict Jesus and His apostles, together with those who were eye and ear witnesses of the facts, as well as the whole Christian Church from then till now! And if they admit that this is baptism, they thereby admit that baptism is administered by pouring—administered by the baptismal element falling upon the parties baptized; and by this admission they concede all we claim, and give up the controversy! Upon one of the horns of this dilemma we suspend all the opposers of baptism by *pouring;* they may choose which they please, for either is fatal to their cause, and they must choose one or the other! If they deny that this is baptism, they are infidels, for Jesus and His apostles say it is; and if they admit that pouring is baptism, they admit all we claim, and the controversy is at an end.

But knowing the obtuseness of those who will not admit of anything short of plunging for baptism, we will add fact to fact, and text to text, if by any means we may convince them of their error, and lead them to an acknowledgment of the truth.

In Acts xi. 15-17, the baptism at the house of Cornelius is thus recorded by Peter: "And as I began to speak, the Holy Ghost fell upon them, as upon us at the beginning. Then remembered I the word of the Lord, how that he said, John indeed baptized with water; but ye shall be baptized with the Holy Ghost. Forasmuch then as God gave them the like gift as He did unto us, who believed on the Lord Jesus Christ, what was I, that I could withstand God?"

Here let the following particulars be noticed. 1. God baptized on this occasion, at the house of Cornelius, in the same way that he baptized at Jerusalem, on the day of Pentecost; 'the Holy Ghost fell on them as He did on us at the beginning." In each case the baptismal element *fell upon them*—they were not plunged in it. 2. The administration in each case is called baptism. John baptized, and God baptized. 3. The latter reminded Peter of the former; therefore, as we know that the latter was by *pouring*, we infer that the *mode* in the former case was the same, for *pouring* could not remind any one of *plunging*. If a Baptist should see one baptizing another by *pouring*, would he say that it reminded him of John baptizing by *plunging* in Jordan? And if such an association of ideas in the mind of a modern Baptist would be considered absurd, and even impossible, let such admit that it would be equally absurd and impossible in the mind of Peter. Thus we are forced to admit that John's baptism *with water* was similar to God's baptism with the Holy Ghost or charge Peter with an association of ideas at once absurd and impossible! Moreover, we KNOW that God baptized by POURING, and we defy any man to prove that John baptized by PLUNGING! Seeing, then, that the latter is *unknown*, to say the least, and the former confessedly KNOWN, common sense says follow the *known* rather than the *unknown;* follow what we KNOW to be God's *mode* of baptizing rather than what we *do not know* to be John's mode! It follows, then, it inevitably follows, that we have this advantage over the immersionists; we follow what we KNOW to be God's *mode* of baptizing, they follow what they cannot prove to be John's mode. And even if they could prove that John administered the rite by plunging, which they can not do, still they must concede to us all we claim, namely: that pouring or sprinkling properly administered is baptism, FOR GOD SAYS IT IS. And even though they could prove that the Apostles administered baptism by plunging, which they can not, still the fact remains, sprinkling or pouring properly administered is baptism, for God says it is, and by pouring He Himself has invariably administered baptism. At best, the claim of the Anabaptists rests upon inference, conjecture, or assumption; ours upon the precept and practice of the Almighty. Nor would it avail if the Anabaptists could prove that John baptized by plunging, for it would not follow that we should, seeing his was not Christian baptism, as we have already shown. It follows, finally, that the Anabaptists must concede that we are right, unless they can prove that God is wrong, for both His teaching and His practice are in favor of sprinkling and pouring. This is fact, not conjecture, not mere inference, not mere assumption!

It really does appear to us that it would be difficult, very difficult, even to conceive of argument more complete than is our argument in favor of baptism by sprinkling or pouring.

We have shown on the testimony of God's own word, that our mode of baptizing is God's mode, while the Anabaptists cannot show that plunging was John's mode; we say they cannot; it is not possible for them to do so. And even if they could, that would not prove that plunging is the right, much less the only mode of Christian baptism; nor would it affect our position at all, for still it would remain a fact, that our mode is God's mode, and that pouring or sprinkling properly administered is baptism, for God says it is; though Anabaptists are bold enough to assert that it is not.

But immersionists even attempt to make it appear

that the baptism "with the Holy Ghost," on the day of Pentecost, was by immersion. They say the Holy Ghost filled the place, therefore all the people in the place were immersed in the Holy Ghost. The passage referred to is Acts ii. 2, and reads thus: "And suddenly there came a sound from heaven, as of a rushing mighty wind, and *it* (the sound, not the Holy Ghost) filled all the house where they were sitting. And there appeared unto them cloven tongues like as of fire, and it sat upon each of them. And they were all filled with the Holy Ghost." Here are four particulars to which we call attention. 1. The sound filled the house where they were sitting. 2. The disciples were filled with the Holy Ghost. 3. The symbol sat upon each of them. 4. And all CAME FROM HEAVEN, *fell upon, sat upon, was shed forth, and filled them.* Here was no *plunging,* nor anything like it. *The sound came from above and filled the place; the spirit came from above and filled the disciples; and the symbol came from above and sat upon each of them;* so that the *mode* here, also, is just the reverse of that claimed by the immersionists: all came from above and fell upon them; they were not plunged into *anything!* And this is what God calls baptism. Defiant of all this, however, *immersionists* assert that *pouring, sprinkling, falling,* is no baptism. God says it is, they say it is not. God affirms, they deny. These are the facts in the case.

We will now group together those terms which God uses in reference to, and in connection with, baptism, and which, it will be seen, absolutely *excludes* the idea of *plunging* in the administration of that ordinance.

John i. 32: "And John bare record, saying, I saw

the Spirit *descending from heaven* like a dove, and it abode upon him." Luke xxiv. 49 : "And behold I send the promise of My Father *upon you:* but tarry ye in the city of Jerusalem, until ye be endued with power *from on high.*" When God baptized with the Holy Ghost on the day of Pentecost, Peter said: "This is that which was spoken by the prophet Joel, And it shall come to pass in the last days, saith God, I will *pour out My Spirit* upon all flesh." See Acts ii. 16, 17. Also at verse 33 we read : "Therefore being at the right hand of God exalted, and having received of the Father the promise of the Holy Ghost, he hath *shed forth* this which ye now see and hear." Acts x. 44: "While Peter yet spake these words the Holy Ghost *fell on* all them which heard the word." Verse 45: "On the Gentiles also was *poured out* the gift of the Holy Ghost." Acts xi. 15: "The Holy Ghost *fell on them,* as on us at the beginning." Titus iii. 5, 6: "But according to His mercy He saved us, by the washing of regeneration, and the renewing of the Holy Ghost; which He *shed on us* abundantly." Acts i. 5 : "For John truly baptized *with* water, but ye shall be baptized *with* the Holy Ghost."

Now it is an indisputable fact that the baptism here spoken of was administered by *descending, shedding, falling, pouring;* not by *plunging!* And, observe, this baptism which was administered by *pouring,* is spoken of in connection with John's baptism: "For John truly baptized *with* water, but ye shall be baptized *with* the Holy Ghost." To say that Christ *plunged the people in the Holy Ghost* would be utterly intolerable, if not blasphemous. And we have no authority to use different terms in each case; God does not; the terms which He uses to express John's administration are the very same that He uses to express His own. John baptized *with* water, He *with* the Holy Ghost. Therefore, as we know that God baptized by *pouring*, we have no right to assume that John or the apostles baptized by *plunging*, and no man living can prove that they did! And, observe, the terms here quoted refer both to the outward and the inward baptism; the outward and the inward *sealing*. The symbol, as well as the thing signified, *fell upon them*. But the advocates of plunging will have the party *plunged in the symbol*. The idea is alike absurd and unscriptural, and therefore could never proceed from God. It certainly is the offspring of ignorance and superstition. Moreover, there is nothing in religion, absolutely nothing, of which *plunging* is the symbol. But pouring is most strikingly symbolical. Hence, as a symbol of the baptism of the Holy Ghost, it has been practiced from time immemorial. Oil, it is well known, was poured upon the heads of high functionaries, as symbolical of the Spirit's descent upon them. But who ever thought of *plunging them in the oil* to signify that thing! The fact is, the more I investigate this subject, the more I become convinced that plunging for the purpose of administering Christian baptism is of human invention; I verily believe that God never appointed it, and I am sure no man can *prove* that he did; but a child can prove that he appointed *pouring* and *sprinkling*, just as soon as he is capable of reading God's book, for there the fact is written so plainly that he that runs may read. And, we may add, it is not likely that God would appoint both *pouring* and *plunging* as symbolical of one and the same thing, for they are entirely dissimilar.

CHAPTER III.

The idea that Christ's baptism and that of Christians are symbolical of Christ's burial, has no countenance from Scripture. It is absurd. Romans vi. 3, 4 fully examined and rescued from their perversions.

I AM aware immersionists would have us believe that a plunge under water is an emblem of the burial of Christ's body. This idea they attempt to express in the following puerile lines:

"In Jordan's flood the prophet stands,
Immersing the returning Jews;
The Son of God the right demands,
Nor dare the Holy Man refuse;
But plunges him beneath the wave,
An emblem of his future grave;
Ye heavens behold the Saviour lie,
Beneath the flood from human eye."

In Matt. xxvii. 60, we are told that "Joseph took the body of Jesus and laid it in his own new tomb, which he had hewn out in the rock." And immersionists tell us that John plunged the living Saviour in the river Jordan as an emblem of this transaction; and they will have us all plunged under water for the same purpose! Truly it requires a marvellous stretch of imagination to discover a resemblance between a dead body being "wrapped in a clean linen cloth" and laid in the cavity of a rock, and a living man walking into a river and being plunged under the water and lifted up again! They certainly must be hard up for a case of resemblance who seek it here; and that they seek it here is sufficient proof of the truth of the statement just made, viz.: that there is nothing in religion of which a sudden plunge under water is the type; for, if there was anything of which it is the most feeble type, they would never attempt to persuade us that it is an emblem of a dead body being laid in the cavity of a rock! for between these two transactions there is simply no resemblance at all. Moreover, we are nowhere taught in Scripture that the design of baptism is to symbolize Christ's body being laid in the tomb.

But immersionists think, or pretend to think, that Paul favors this view, Rom. vi. 3, 4. The whole passage reads thus. "Know ye not that so many of us as were baptized into Jesus Christ, were baptized into his death? Therefore we are buried with him by baptism into death: That like as Christ was raised up from the dead by the glory of the Father, even so we also should walk in newness of life. For if we have been planted together in the likeness of his death, we shall be also in the likeness of his resurrection: knowing this, that our old man is crucified with him, that the body of sin might be destroyed, that henceforth we should not serve sin."

Immersionists say, that, to be baptized is to be *plunged*, and that the word "means neither more nor less." Hence they would read this passage thus: "Know ye not that so many of us as were *plunged* into Jesus Christ, were *plunged* into his death?" Such language is, of course, utterably intolerable; hence it is evident that to baptize does not mean to plunge: and it is equally evident that the Apostle in this passage has no reference at all to the *mode* of baptism. Therefore, as immersionists build their argument upon this assumption, the foundation being taken away the argument becomes worthless, or rather is no argument at all. Of this difficulty they evidently are conscious, for although the Apostle uses three figures in the same connection, immersionists never notice any but one of them, viz. that of *burying ;* whereas the apostle speaks of our being *buried*, *planted* and *crucified*. Now why do they not insist upon a *mode* of baptism that will symbolize *planting* and *crucifying* as well as *burying ?* for it is quite evident that the passage countenances all three as much as it does either one. The fact is, it is impossible to adopt a mode of baptism that will symbolize either : Nor was it ever designed that we should. This is evident from the fact that the outward and visible sign in a sacrament is always symbolical of something spiritual ; but if you make water baptism the sign of the crucifixion and burial of Christ, you make the literal to represent the literal, the symbol to symbolize the symbol, which is absurd ! Yet this is the very thing that immersionists do by their unnatural and forced interpretation of this highly figurative passage. Christ's dead body was laid in the cavity of a rock, and they say baptism by plunging is symbolical of that !

By this interpretation of the passage before us the design of the Apostle is wholly lost sight of. The manifest design of the Apostle is to show that justification by faith does not lead to licentiousness in the life of the believer.

Having established the doctrine of justification by faith he proceeds to meet the objection of its opponents thus. " Shall we continue in sin that grace may abound ?

God forbid : how shall we that are dead to sin, live any longer therein." So far from continuing in sin the believer is DEAD to sin. This is the Apostle's answer to the objection. And this death to sin, or crucifixion of the old man, he represents as brought about by the death of Christ, and the baptism of the Holy Ghost, with faith on our part; of which faith, water baptism is the appropriate outward expression; and, at the same time, the seal of the righteousness thus procured, as well as the sign of the baptism by the Spirit. "Then," says Mr. Watson, (Institutes, vol. ii. p. 658,) "he immediately runs into a favorite comparison, which, under various forms, occurs in his writings, sometimes accompanied with the same allusion to baptism, and sometimes referring only to faith as the instrument, a comparison between the mystical death, burial, and resurrection of believers and the literal death, burial, and resurrection of Christ. This is the comparison of the text; not a comparison between our mystical death and baptism; nor between baptism and the death and burial of Christ; either of which lay wide of the Apostle's intention." Any one who will read from the 6th to the 11th verse of this chapter, will see that this is the comparison that the Apostle employs for the purpose specified. "Knowing this," says the Apostle, "that our old man is crucified with him, that the body of sin might be destroyed, that henceforth we should not serve sin. For he that is dead is freed from sin. Now if we be dead with Christ we believe that we shall also live with him : Knowing that Christ, being raised from the dead, dieth no more; death hath no more dominion over him. For in that he died, he died unto sin once; but in that he liveth, he liveth unto God. Likewise reckon ye also yourselves to be dead indeed unto sin, but alive unto God through Jesus Christ our Lord."

The sublime and glorious sentiments of the Apostle here expressed are briefly these: the believer is "dead to sin" and is "thus freed from sin;" and his former unholy connection with the world is thus as effectually dissolved, as is our literal connection with the world by a literal death. And the comparison is between this mystical death and separation, and Christ's death; by which *his* literal connection with the world was dissolved, and our death to sin and freedom from sin secured; and, in this way, our unholy connection with the world is as effectually dissolved, as was Christ's literal connection with the world, by his literal death. Now having compared our mystical death and separation from the world, to Christ's literal death and separation from the world, he continues the train of thought and proceeds to compare our mystical resurrection to Christ's literal resurrection, thus: "That like as Christ was raised from the dead by the glory of the Father, even so we also should walk in newness of life. For if we have been planted together in the likeness of his death, we shall be also in the likeness of his resurrection. Knowing this, that our old man is crucified with him, that the body of sin might be destroyed, that henceforth we should not serve sin. For he that is dead is freed from sin. Now if we be dead with Christ we believe that we shall also live with him. For in that he died, he died unto sin once: but in that he liveth, he liveth unto God. Likewise reckon ye also yourselves to be dead indeed unto sin, but alive unto God through Jesus Christ our Lord."

Now to represent the Apostle in all these his sublime

and inspired conceptions, illustrations and arguments, as simply attempting a comparison between plunging living men and women under water, and laying Christ's dead body in a tomb hewn out of a rock, is to degrade this noble and inspired production into driveling nonsense, and absolutely ignore the noble and glorious end or ends which he had in view, namely, to show the nature and extent of that change wrought in the sinner upon his believing in Jesus; together with the manner, or way, in which it is wrought, and thus refute the slanderous objection raised against the doctrine of justification by faith, viz., that it leads to a licentious life. And thus it is that error always leads from the truth and becomes a substitute for it; and in this case a very pernicious substitute!

CHAPTER IV.

The word sprinkle is now taken up—Its use and design shown from Scripture—Plunging for the purpose of sealing is an outrage upon common sense.

HAVING rescued from the perversions of the Anabaptists the much abused words *baptized*, *buried*; we now take up the word *sprinkle*.

This word occurs with great frequency, and in the same connection, both in the Old and New Testament. We will here quote a few of the passages in which it occurs. Levit. xiv. 1, 2: "And the LORD spake unto Moses, saying, This shall be the law of the leper in the day of his cleansing."—"And he shall sprinkle upon him that is to be cleansed from the leprosy seven times," ver. 4. At ver. 15–18 we read, "And the priest shall take some of the log of oil and pour it into the palm of his own left hand: and the priest shall dip his right finger into the oil that is in his left hand, and shall sprinkle of the oil with his finger seven times before the Lord."—"And the remnant of the oil that is in the priest's hand he shall pour upon the head of him that is to be cleansed." Now the oil and blood here spoken of were used for the same purpose that water is used for in the sacrament of baptism, viz., as a sign; and a little in the palm of the hand, sprinkled with the tip of one finger, God considered quite sufficient; but Anabaptists think it quite ridiculous to use so small a quantity ; instead of sprinkling the individual with the oil, blood, or water, they would have him plunged in it! But we will quote a few more passages. Levit. xvi. 14, "And he shall take of the blood of the bullock, and sprinkle it with his finger upon the mercy-seat." Numbers viii. 7, "And thus shalt thou do unto them to cleanse them: sprinkle water of purifying upon them!" Numbers xix. 18, "And a clean person shall take hyssop, and dip it in the water, and sprinkle it upon the tent, and upon all the vessels, and upon the persons that were there." Thus were they to do "for an unclean person;" and everybody knows, or should know, that baptism with water has reference to moral uncleanness, and to the same thing circumcision referred, and as neither blood nor water could cleanse the soul, but was applied to the body merely as a sign, a few drops sprinkled with the finger answered the purpose. The fact is, the idea of virtue is attached to the outward application by all those who object to small, and contend for large, quantities of water; and in this way the ordinance is perverted and vitiated, and the inward application, which is the thing signified, and which alone possesses the cleansing power, is wholly lost sight of: and this, in our judgment, is a serious objection to the practice of plunging instead of sprinkling or pouring. But there really is no excuse for thus losing the spirit in the letter, for God has made the design of the outward application sufficiently plain, as the following quotations will show. Isaiah lii. 15, "So shall he [Jesus] sprinkle many nations." Ezekiel xxxvi. 25—27, "Then will I sprinkle clean water upon you, and ye shall be clean: from all your filthiness, and from all your idols, will I cleanse you. A new heart also will I give you, and a new spirit will I put within you: and I will take away the stony heart out of your flesh, and I will give you an heart of flesh. And I will put my Spirit within you, and cause you to walk in my statutes, and ye shall keep my judgments, and do them." Heb. ix. 19, "For when Moses had spoken every precept to all the people according to the law, he took the blood of calves and of goats, with water, and scarlet wool, and hyssop, and sprinkled both the book and all the people." Heb. x. 22, "Let us draw near with a true heart, in full assurance of faith, having our hearts sprinkled from an evil conscience." Heb. xii. 24, "*We* are come to Jesus the mediator of the new covenant, and to the blood of sprinkling that speaketh better things than that of Abel."

Thus all these sprinklings end in that which they typify, namely, the sprinkling, the cleansing of the soul by the blood of Jesus: and a few drops answered this purpose as well as a river, or a sea, and much better; but man, poor, ignorant, carnal man, must improve upon God's way of it; instead of having the sign or seal applied to the person, he, forsooth, must have the person plunge in it: the idea is unnatural and absurd in the extreme! Baptism is a sign and seal, as circumcision was; and, of course, the seal should be applied to the party to be sealed, not the party to the seal! It is thus that God uses the seal, as the foregoing Scriptures do most incontestibly show. And the following text affords still more striking evidence, if that be possible. "After that ye believed ye were sealed with the Holy Spirit of promise."—Ep. i. 13. It is obvious that the Apostle here speaks of the same baptism, the same sealing, which was the subject of promise in the texts quoted above. "I will pour out my Spirit upon you," "Ye shall be baptized with the Holy Ghost." It is to this promise that the Apostle refers when he says. "After that ye believed ye were sealed with the Holy Spirit of promise." The symbol fell upon the body, the Spirit upon the soul. So it is in the administration of the sacrament of baptism : the symbol, the seal, which is water, falls upon and seals the body, the Spirit falls upon and seals the soul. This, then, is another ground of objection to plunging. God's method, or mode, of baptizing includes, and very strikingly expresses, the idea of *sealing*, while plunging utterly excludes that idea ; the idea of plunging for the purpose of sealing is an outrage on common sense.

CHAPTER V.

The assumption that *en*, *eis*, and *ek*, always mean in, into, and out of, is refuted, and the argument built thereon, shown to be worthless, a mere begging of the question.

We now take up the argument which immersionists ground upon the *assumption* that the Greek prepositions *en*, *eis*, and *ek*, always mean *in*, *into*, and *out of*. On this assumption it is confidently asserted that John baptized *in* Jordan, that Jesus came up *out of* the water, and that Philip and the Eunuch went down *into* the water, and came up *out of* the water, and, finally, that they must all have been plunged under the water! Hence this famous argument is made up of *three assumptions*, viz., that these words mean what immersionists say they mean, neither more nor less; second, that all the parties mentioned went *into* the water and were baptized *in it;* third, that, therefore, they must all have been plunged under the water. Now in all this there is absolutely nothing but assumption, which assumption we now proceed to disprove.

We will first take up the preposition *en*. Now, observe, we do not deny that the Greek word *en* sometimes means *in;* but we do deny that it always has this meaning. Mr. Thorne says, "From an accurate investigation of the subject," he finds that, "in our version of the New

Testament, the translators have rendered *en*, *at*, *on*, or *with*, three hundred and thirteen times. But lest the immersionist should say that our translators should have rendered *en*, *in*, in all these places, we will quote a few passages, which will, we think, demonstrate that it would be highly improper, in many instances to render *en*, *in*. And here I beg to state that I have examined the original for myself, and am prepared to say that it reads as I here state. Matt. iii. 11. "I indeed baptize you *en* water *eis* repentance: but he that cometh after me is mightier than I, whose shoes I am not worthy to bear: he shall baptize you *en* the Holy Ghost, and fire." Now let *en*, and *eis*, in this passage be rendered *in*, and *into*, and then the passage will read thus, "I indeed baptize you *in* water *into* repentance:"—"but he shall baptize you *in* the Holy Ghost and fire." And if we render *baptize*, *plunge*, in this text, as immersionists say we should, the case will be still worse: then the text will read, "I indeed plunge you *in* water *into* repentance:"—"but he shall plunge you *in* the Holy Ghost and fire." Now in addition to the absurdity, not to say blasphemy, of this rendering, it leaves us without any baptism at all, either literal or spiritual; *nothing but plunging* IN *water* INTO *repentance and* IN *the Holy Ghost!* By this exhibit any one can see the absurdity and the untruthfulness of the assumption here opposed. Take another instance. In Romans viii. 34, we read, "Who is he that condemneth? It is Christ that died, yea, rather, that is risen again, who is even *at* the right hand of God." The word here rendered *at* is, in the original, in one of my Greek Testaments *en*, in the other *eis*. Now according to the assumption here opposed, this text would read, in the one, "who is even *in* the right hand of God," and in the other, "who is even *into* the right hand of God!" This presents the absurdity and untruthfulness of the assumption with similar clearness. We have examined many other texts where this preposition means *at*, *by*, *near to*. See, for instance, Luke xiii. 4, where our Lord speaks of "the Tower *en* Siloam." Certainly the tower was not in the pool, or well, but at or near it. In one of my Greek Testaments the words are, "Ho purgos *eis* to Siloam;" "the tower *into* Siloam," according to the assumption here opposed! In Matt. ix. 35, we are told Christ "healed every sickness, and every disease among the people." The word here rendered *among*, is in the original *en*, and in one of my Greek Testaments *eis*, hence according to the claims of immersionists this text should read, "every sickness and every disease *in*, or *into*, the people! Let these few out of many texts suffice to show the untruthfulness and the absurdity of the assumption here objected to, and we think now fully refuted.

The preposition *eis* may now come under notice. The arguments in favor of immersion are based on the assumption that this word always means *into*. In Matt. xxi. 1, we read "And when they drew nigh unto Jerusalem, and were come to Bethphage, unto the Mount of Olives." Here *eis* is rendered *nigh*, with regard to the one place, and *to* with regard to the other, for it is evident Jesus and his companions could not enter both places at the same time, they being distant from each other. In Matt. xvii. 27, Peter is commanded to "go *eis* the sea, and cast an hook." It is evident that Peter is not here commanded to go *into* the sea to cast in thither his hook; to cast a hook into the sea at Capernaum it was not necessary that he should go into the sea, probably not practicable; hence our translators have rendered *eis*, *to*, not *into*, and they had as much authority so to translate in the narrative of John's baptism, and that of Philip: and immersionists have no more right to place John in Jordan, and Philip and the Eunuch in the water, than they have to place Peter in the sea at Capernaum.

Acts xxiv. 15. "And have hope *toward* God," not *into* God. Matt. xviii. 15. "If thy brother shall trespass *against* thee," here *eis* is rendered against, for it would not be proper to say trespassed *into* thee, any more than it would have been proper to say in the former text, hope *into* God. Mark iii. 29. "But he that shall blaspheme *against* the Holy Ghost." Here again *eis* is rendered *against*, for it certainly would not be proper to say "blaspheme *into* the Holy Ghost." Acts xxii. 30. "Brought Paul and set him *before* them." Here *eis* is rendered *before*, for it would not be proper to say, set him *into* them. In Isaiah xxxvi. 2, we read, "And the King of Assyria sent Rabshakeh from Lachish to Jerusalem." In the Septuagint the reading is *ek* Lachish *eis* Jerusalem. Here it is evident that *ek* and *eis* mean *from* and *to*, not *out of*, and *into*, for Rabshakeh was not sent *into* Jerusalem. And we have the same authority to translate *to* the water, and *from* the water, in the narrative of the Eunuch's baptism by Philip. In short, every scholar knows that both sacred and classic writers use *ek*, and *eis*, to express the ideas *from*, and *to*. *Apo* and *eis* are also used in the same connection: hence we read, *apo* city *eis* city. That is, from city to city. *Apo* Jerusalem, *eis* Jericho. Also, the way that goeth down *apo* Jerusalem, *eis* Gaza. That is, "the way that goeth down from Jerusalem to Gaza."

With regard to *ek*, or *ex*, we will simply quote a few texts to show the various meanings of that preposition. Matt. xii. 33. "The tree is known *by* its fruit." Here *ek* is rendered *by*. Matt. xx. 2. "Agreed with the laborers *ek denariou*;" that is, *for* a penny. In Matt. xxi. 19, it is rendered *on*; in Rom. ix. 21, it is rendered *of*. In short, Mr. Thorne, who has been at the trouble of counting, tells us that in the New Testament *ek* is rendered *from*, 186 times, and *eis to*, or *unto*, 538 times. And in Schleusner's Lexicon of the New Testament, we are told that *ek* has 24 distinct meanings, or senses, *en* 36, and *eis* 26. And yet the advocates of *plunging*, as the only mode of baptism, build their arguments upon the *assumption* that *en*, *eis*, and *ek*, always mean *in*, *into*, and *out of*. It is true, they admit, at least those of them who are scholars, that these words have a great variety of meanings; but it is equally true that the arguments which they deduce from the narratives of John's and Philip's baptism are all based upon this assumption. Indeed they admit that the word *baptizo* has a great variety of meanings, yet, strange as it may appear, their arguments in favor of plunging are, for the most part, built upon the assumption that it always means "to immerse, to dip, to plunge, neither more nor less." But that this assumption is without warrant or plausibility we believe we have clearly shown. Nor will the connection in which the word *baptizo* is found in the Scriptures give any countenance to this assumption; for it is found connected with the words *fall*, *pour*, *shed*, *sprinkle*, and other words of similar import. And with regard to the prepositions with which it sometimes stands connected, we trust we have shown that they give no warrant for the assumption: therefore the assumption is utterly without foundation! And, let it be distinctly observed, that, at the very most, there can be no more than assumption; for no man in his senses can claim that we are anywhere in the Scriptures commanded to plunge in the name of the Father, and of the Son, and of the Holy Ghost! The utmost that can be claimed, even with the slightest plausibility, by the advocates of plunging, is that the verb baptizo sometimes means to plunge; but even if we admit this claim, our admission will not affect our position, for still it will remain a fact that sprinkling or pouring is baptism, for God says it is, and in that way he always administers baptism: nor would our admission afford the advocates of plunging any help till they first prove that the word has that meaning in Scripture where Christian baptism is recorded and enjoined; and this we know they cannot do, while we can prove, and have proved, that it means to sprinkle, to pour, and that this is God's mode, INVARIABLY SO. Once again I say, and I say it with all confidence, that no man living can prove that God ever taught plunging for baptism; hence those who undertake to administer baptism in that way do it upon their own authority. And everybody knows, or may know, that God never baptized by plunging! Here are the facts: God's precept is pouring; his practice is pouring; while in favor of plunging there is absolutely not one jot or tittle! Let them disprove this conclusion who can.

CHAPTER VI.

A fallacy and its terrible consequences exposed. If Philip and the Eunuch did go down into the water it would not follow that either was plunged—The question, "why did John baptize where there was much water?" answered.

JUST here it may be well to expose the fallacy and show the terrible consequences, of taking that which is occasionally the meaning of a given word, and assuming that such is its *primary*, its *only* meaning.

The primary meaning of the Greek word *doulos* is, *poor*, *exhausted*, *reduced to poverty*. Hence this word was used to designate a *servant*, and finally a *slave*. Now take the latter as the primary, the only meaning of the word *doulos*, and you may prove that all who are employed by their fellow men are *slaves*, yea, and that all the people of God are *slaves!* It is in this way that slaveholders, and the advocates of slavery, have attempted to prove that slavery is of divine appointment, is scriptural, because in the scriptures certain directions are given to regulate the mutual relations and obligations of *kurioi* and *douloi;* that is, masters and servants. Again the primary meaning of the word *pistis*, is *faith*, but it sometimes means *fidelity*. Now assume that the latter is its only meaning and you may prove that salvation is not by believing, but by fidelity, and in this way you would overturn the whole Christian system! Again the primary meaning of the Greek word *pneuma*, like the Hebrew word *ruach*, is spirit, but it sometimes means, *wind, air*. Now only assume that the latter is its only meaning and you may prove from the Bible that God is the wind, for our blessed Lord says *Pneuma ho Theos*, that is, according to this assumption, God is the wind! In the same way you may prove that man's higher nature is mere wind or air! Again *psuche* means the immortal part of man as distinguished from the body; but it sometimes means the breath, and even the blood, because these are the essential of animal life, and the primary meaning of *psuche* being life, it is applied thereto in a secondary sense; but its primary application is to the immortal part, that being life in the highest sense. Now if you take the accommodated meaning of this word and assume that to be its only meaning, you will reach the conclusion of the Adventists, or Nasoulites, viz., that man has no soul, no spirit, that there is nothing of him but mere matter. Again *deipnon* means a supper, a common meal, a feast; assume this to be the only meaning of the word and like the Corinthians you will reduce "the Lord's supper" to a common meal, a feast. Once more. The Hebrew word *Sheol* and the Greek word Hades mean the hidden, the concealed, the lowest place, or condition; hence it is applied to the grave. Now let it be assumed that the latter is the only meaning of the word, and you will reach the conclusion, with the universalist, that there is no hell, no punishment or place of punishment, in the other world.

Now, this is precisely the fallacy which, to the ignorant, gives plausibility to what immersionists say in favor of their mode of baptizing. They say *en* means *in*, *eis* means into, and *ek* means out of, and so they do; but, assuming that these are the only meanings of these words, and finding them used sometimes, though not always, in the narrative of John's baptism, and that by Philip, they say they went down into the water and came up out of it, ergo, they baptized by plunging! Now, in precisely the same way others conclude that man is a mere animal, and that there is no future punishment. Such is the nature of this fallacy, and such are the terrible consequences to which it leads, or may lead the ignorant and unsuspecting.

Having shown that the Greek prepositions, *en, eis*, and *ek*, are employed both by the sacred and classic writers to express the ideas *near*, *to*, and *from*, and many others, as well as *in*, *into*, and *out of*, we have disproved the assumption of the immersionists, viz., that they always mean in, into, and out of; and as many of their arguments in favor of plunging rest upon this assumption, it follows that such arguments are worthless: hence all their conclusions in favor of immersion, so far as they depend upon the statements that John baptized *in* Jordan, and that Philip and the Eunuch went down *into* the water and came *up out of it*, are illegitimate and worthless; therefore, if they would prove *plunging* to be the right *mode* they must derive their proof from a very different source, for every scholar knows that the Greek prepositions afford no such proof.

But even though they could prove that Philip and the Eunuch went down into the water, that would not prove that the latter was plunged under the water, for if Philip baptized the Eunuch by sprinkling, they would both have to go to or into the water to this end, for it is not likely that they had a vessel with them to carry water to a distance, and it is still less likely that the water would come up to them in the chariot. Moreover, if the text proves that the Eunuch was immersed, it also proves that Philip was immersed; for there is nothing said of the one, with regard to going down and coming up, that is not said of the other. In short, the language employed to record this event, is just such as any one would employ where immersion was not so much as thought of. It should be observed, too, that if the Eunuch was immersed he must have been immersed naked, or with his clothes on, for it is not likely that he had a change of garments with him, nor is it at all likely that he would pursue his long journey in the garments in which he was plunged in the water, and he did pursue his journey immediately after being baptized, for we are told, "when they were come up out of," or from "the water, the Spirit of the Lord caught away Philip, that the Eunuch saw him no more, and he went on his way rejoicing." I should think he would feel more like trembling than rejoicing, if he was sitting in the chariot in the same clothes in which he had just before been plunged under water; and there certainly is no intimation of his having undressed, and dressed again. In short, there is nothing in this narrative that would lead any one to the belief that Philip plunged the Eunnch under water, especially when it is remembered that the divinely instituted method of *pouring* and *sprinkling* had existed among Philip's ancestors for nearly two thousand years! Indeed, the prophecy which Philip was explaining to the Eunuch, and which led to the conversion and baptism of the latter, contains these remarkable words: "So shall he sprinkle many nations." See last verse of chap. 52 of Isaiah. Being now a believer in him who should "sprinkle many nations," the Eunuch at once desired to be baptized, agreeably to the prophetic promise now before him, and which Philip was explaining to him. Now, as sprinkling, not plunging, was specified in the passage before them, and as that mode had been practised by the Jews from the first until now, and that by divine appointment, it is not likely that either Philip or the Eunuch would think of plunging on this occasion The Eunuch said: "I pray thee, of whom speaketh the prophet this?" Philip told him that it was Jesus of whom the prophet spake, and the Eunuch believed. The prophet said that this Jesus would "sprinkle many nations;" and the Eunuch said: "See, here is water, what doth hinder me to be baptized?" There was nothing to hinder him—he was baptized, by sprinkling, doubtless, agreeably to the scripture, upon which they had just now been meditating.

It is only necessary to add, that all we have said with regard to the baptism by Philip, will apply to John's baptism, and is a sufficient answer to the arguments which the advocates of immersion employ to prove that John plunged the people under water; for their arguments in each case are derived from the same assumption, viz.: that *eis*, *en*, and *ek* mean *into*, *in*, and *out of*. Indeed it is not said in the original that Jesus came up out of the water. In Matt. iii. 16, the original reads: *anebē euphus apo tou hudatos*, *up straight* FROM *the water*. Therefore, with regard to John's baptism it only remains for us to answer the question, "If John did not immerse why did he baptize where there was much water?" We reply, if your mind were not unduly occupied with the dogma of immersion you would find a satisfactory answer to your question in the sacred narrative. Just read the following: And he came into all the country about Jordan preaching the baptism of repentance for the remission of sins." Here follow specimens of his preaching and of his exhortations. Luke iii. 3: "Then went out to him Jerusalem, and all Judea, and all the region round about Jordan." Matt. iii. 5: "John did baptize in the wilderness, and preach the baptism of repentance for the remission of sins." Observe, it is not only said that he "baptized in Jordan," but also that he "baptized in the wilderness." Hence, I have as good a right to infer from these texts that John *plunged* in the wilderness as others have to infer that he plunged in Jordan, the same preposition being used in each case. In one of my Greek Testaments the words are *eis ten erēmon,* in the other *en te erēmō.*

But my special object in quoting these texts is to call attention to the vast multitudes which came to John from Jerusalem and the different regions here specified, certainly not less than several millions, with their camels, &c., to abide there for a length of time to be instructed by the great preacher who was the forerunner of their long expected Messiah, and who was now preparing them for his immediate coming. It is quite evident that such vast multitudes under such circumstances, required much water for domestic and other purposes. In short, no man in his senses would bring such multitudes of human beings and beasts of burden from a distance to abide for a time where there was *not much* water; especially in a hot season, and in a country where water generally was scarce. Moreover, if he was to preach to and baptize the people dwelling in "all the region round about Jordan," it was obviously proper that he should have his station at Jordan, that being a central position. For similar reasons he had his station at another time at Enon, where there was a suitable supply of water; though there does not appear to have been the vast quantities that immersionists would have us believe there was; for travellers find no evidence of there being in Enon any more than certain fountains or springs. It is well known that camp-meetings in this country are always held where there is plenty of water, though I suppose a thousand such congregations would not be equal to the vast multitudes who came to hear this great preacher in the wilderness, and to be baptized of him. From these considerations it is evident that John needed much water for the millions to whom he preached in the wilderness, without supposing that he plunged them all into it! The idea is as gratuitous as it is extravagant. How is it that we never hear of the apostles baptizing where much water was? Evidently because they labored where the people were at or near their homes, and, therefore, had all the necessaries of domestic life; and, there being no plunging, that was sufficient.

CHAPTER VII.

The dogma that nothing but Plunging is Baptism is shown to involve what is Unreasonable, Inhuman, and even Impossible.

We must not pass unnoticed the *unreasonableness* of the assumptions here objected to. For instance, is it reasonable to suppose that one man plunged millions of people in a river, "in the wilderness," where neither himself nor the millions thus plunged had any home or any of the conveniences of domestic life? Is it reasonable to suppose that all these vast multitudes had changes of raiment or gowns for the purpose? or that they were plunged into the river having on them the only suit of clothes they had? or that the countless multitudes should live in the wilderness with their wet garments on till they dried upon their persons? or is it reasonable to suppose that these vast multitudes were exposed and plunged into the river naked? Is it reasonable to suppose that John himself was naked, or that he lived and labored in his wet clothes, or had a sufficient number of changes of raiment of "camel's hair?" Is it reasonable to suppose that any man could live in the wilderness, or, rather, *in the river*, and plunge under water such vast multitudes of people from Jerusalem, from Judea, and from "all the region round about Jordan?" When a man baptizes a few in a river in these days he is glad to hasten to his comfortable home and change as quickly as possible; and the poor trembling female must be carried home in a carriage, or to the nearest house, and stripped as quickly as possible; or if there are a dozen or twenty to be baptized it will require several Sabbaths to do this little work, because a sufficient number of *gowns* cannot be procured! I wonder how long it would have taken John to baptize several millions in this way! Is it reasonable to suppose that a few apostles plunged three thousand men and women on the day of Pentecost, not in Jordan or in Enon, where much water was, but in Jerusalem, where little water was, and all this in a few hours at most; for most of the day was evidently occupied by preaching and other religious exercises? Is it reasonable to suppose that God has made plunging so essential that there can be no baptism, no admission to the sacrament of the supper, no admission into the Christian church, yea, no church at all, without it; although there are countries where water cannot be had unless in very small quantities by melting the snow, for large bodies of water are covered over with ice fifteen or twenty feet thick, while multitudes of others live in dry and parched deserts "where no water is?" Is it reasonable to suppose that an infinitely wise, kind, and merciful God would exclude from the sacrament of baptism, from the sacrament of the supper, and from the Church itself, millions of the feeble, the sick and the wounded; simply because they are in a state which renders it imprudent, yea wicked, and even impossible, to plunge them under water, when his own instituted method may be adopted without risk to the feeblest of them? For instance, thousands of our wounded, sick and mangled soldiers, are obtaining salvation by faith in our adorable Jesus. Must they be deprived of the sacraments, of the seal of the covenant of grace, and shut out from the Church of God, simply because their poor mangled and sick bodies cannot be plunged under water? I ask, is all this scriptural? Is it reasonable? Is it humane? Is it not rather cruel and absurd? Yet all this is implied, is included, in the claims of the immersionists!

CHAPTER VIII.

The appeal to antiquity is simply superstition, cruelty, and absurdity, appealing to superstition, cruelty, and absurdity—Many superstitious and absurd opinions and practices specified as having obtained in the nominally Christian Church at a very early period—It is difficult to mention any one religious dogma that is more clogged with difficulties than is the dogma of plunging.

But, to support these unscriptural, unreasonable, inhuman and cruel claims, immersionists appeal to antiquity. This is none other than superstition, cruelty, and absurdity, appealing to superstition, cruelty, and absurdity for help! What absurdity is there that may not claim kindred with antiquity? Not being satisfied with the simplicity of the divine institutions, men soon began to add to them to make them more impressive. And this work commenced even before the apostles were called away. But as early as the latter end of the second, or the beginning of the third century, the practice of washing before pouring was adopted; then partially immersing followed by pouring; then immersing three times, annointing with oil, signing with the sign of the cross; imposition of hands, exorcism, eating milk and honey, putting on white robes, and other superstitious observances worthy of the dark ages. As early as the third century some, in receiving the sacrament of the supper mixed water with the wine; others used water only; while others used bread and cheese. The Ophites had a tamed serpent which they caused to twine round the bread, then they kissed the serpent and afterwards partook of the bread. The Zanzalians contended that the scriptural baptism was a baptism with fire; and their mode was to brand three times with a red hot iron. The Jovinians taught that grace received in baptism could never be lost. The Hieraxites taught that all infants would be damned, for they held that the procuring cause of salvation was knowledge; and this of course left no chance for the poor infant! The Novatians taught many absurdities, and being confident that they only were right, they, of course, re-baptized all who joined them, and who had been baptized before. The Valentinians baptized in the name of the Father, his Son, and the mother of the world! And as to the Donatists, they taught that baptism administered by any but their own party was invalid, and that they had authority to remove all errors and corruptions from the Church! Now all these and numerous other errors and absurdities, and even blasphemies, were taught in the second, third, and fourth centuries. Nor were these errors confined to the vile sects such as those noticed above, but what was called the orthodox church soon became deluged with pernicious errors and superstitious rights and ceremonies; and many of the leading ministers, such as Tertullian, Origen, and Augustine, largely contributed thereto! Such men were zealous, and swayed the masses with their eloquence, but they were miserable theologians. And why? I answer, because they relied upon their own ability and upon human philosophy to learn and teach what only can be learned and taught from the word of God. Moreover, many of them still clung to errors which they had contracted before they embraced Christianity. Such was the case, for instance, with Augustine, who had been a Manichean before he embraced Christianity. And such was the case with many others who still retained some of their former errors, and embraced others; all of which they attempted to incorporate with the Christian system. But it is useless to dwell upon this feature of antiquity. It is well known that the nominally Christian Church became corrupt at a very early period. "The ancient Christians," says Wall, "when they were baptized by immersion, were all baptized naked, whether they were men, women, or children. They thought it better represented the putting off of the old man, and also the nakedness of Christ on the cross; moreover, as baptism is a washing, they judged it should be the washing of the body, notof the clothes." "There is no ancient historical fact," says Robinson, "better authenticated than this." Now when immersionists appeal to antiquity in favor of immersion, why don't they faithfully follow antiquity, and baptize men, women, and children NAKED? But so far are they from following antiquity that they do not baptize either men or women naked, and as for children, they do not baptize them at all, either naked or clothed; and yet they boast of following antiquity, and loudly complain that we do not copy after their example! Well, while we regret that they follow antiquity in some things, let us be thankful that they do not in others, for we certainly do not wish them to follow antiquity as to the *naked mode!* We, however, think it would be much wiser for them to follow the Bible and let antiquity go, or only follow it as far as it followed Christ!

Now if immersionists infer the practice of John the Baptist, and that of the apostles, from the practice of the

Christians of the third and fourth centuries, they must of course reach the conclusion that John and the apostles *baptized men, women, and children naked!* And if so, a marvellous scene must have been presented at Jordan, and Enon, in the days of John; and a still more marvellous scene must have been presented in Jerusalem on the day of Pentecost. We leave it to your imagination to depict the scene! The following quotation from Wall, however, will somewhat relieve the difficulty. "They, however, took great care for preserving the modesty of any woman who was to be baptized. None but women came near till her body was in the water; then the priest came, and putting her head also under water, he departed and left her to the women." If this was the method on the day of Pentecost, when three thousand persons were baptized, the good sisters in Jerusalem must have had a busy time of it; for we may safely presume that sixteen or eighteen hundred of them were females, for in a revival there are usually more females than males converted. Before this day there were only a very few Christian women in Jerusalem, and we may presume that they were the only women that would attend to this work; and these few women, according to this showing, must have immersed the bodies of some sixteen hundred women, while the apostles only popped their heads under the water, and then left them to the women who put them in to take them out again, and dress them. There was no body of water in Jerusalem in which three thousand could be immersed, neither could they be immersed in one, or even in fifty baths, in a few hours; therefore, if they were immersed at all it must have been in very many baths, in different and distant parts of the city;

then the question arises, how could a few apostles run all over the city, from bath to bath, to immerse three thousand in a few hours? for they "were added to the church the same day." Moreover, most of these baths or cisterns were in the hands of Jews, who were the deadly enemies of the Christians, and would not be likely to let the Christians have their baths. But a still greater difficulty presents itself just here. How could the few Christian females who were then in the city run from bath to bath, all over the city, and put, say, sixteen hundred females into them, and take them out again and dress them, after the apostles had put their heads under? How could they do all this in a few hours? Now it is evident that the advocates of immersion must account for these, or for still greater difficulties. It should be observed, too, that the women baptized the bodies of the women, while the apostles, on this hypothesis, only baptized their heads! Here, too, another question arises, viz., which part of the performance was most orthodox, that of the women, or that of the apostles? One might say of them as Socrates said of living and dying, "which is best the gods know," for I suppose even immersionists themselves cannot tell. And, by the way, there is a similar difficulty connected with modern immersion; for the priest only plunges about one half of the body, while the individual immerses the other half by walking into the water, so that there is only partial immersion by the priest after all; and still the question remains to be decided, which part of the body received scripture baptism? Or did either? The advocates of plunging will please answer!

It is really difficult to mention any one religious dogma that is more clogged with *difficulties* and *absurdities* than is this dogma of *exclusive immersion:* nor does it stop with *difficulties* and *absurdities*, for, as we have seen, it includes positive *impossibilities!*

CHAPTER IX.

Summing up—A great variety of Particulars are Specified—Plunging was, and is, connected with Superstition and various Errors, and is doubtless the Offspring of Superstition—Proselyting, causing Proselytes to Renounce their Baptism is very serious—Unreasonableness of the supposition that the German Fanatics discovered what all the wise and the learned both ancient and modern have failed to discover—It is the duty of Zion's Watchmen to Save their People from being Proselyted—The sincerity of the Anabaptists in crying for Union under certain circumstances is very questionable while they teach as they do—We are not at liberty to reject a Divinely appointed Method and adopt another, especially when that other is very objectionable in itself—Nor is the Church at Liberty to leave to the choice and whims of Men to Decide where it is her duty to Teach what God has already Decided—Taylor's Pictorial Representations showing the Ancient mode of Baptism.

AND now, having said this much, we may sum up the evidence and rest our cause. The amount is briefly this: God's mode of baptizing is by *pouring*, *shedding*, *sprinkling*. In a word, by the baptismal element *falling upon* the party baptized, *invariably so!* this, with all who believe the word of God, is an indisputable fact. Second. In the word of God *that* is called baptism where water *fell upon* the Israelites, and upon Nebuchadnezzar, by *sprinkling* or by *pouring:* this, too, is a fact! Third. There is not in all God's word so much as one clear text in favor of *plunging*, as being the divinely appointed mode of baptism; this, too, is a fact! Fourth. God has appointed sprinkling or pouring, as the appropriate sign of baptism by the Spirit, and as the appropriate sign of cleansing by the blood of Jesus; this, also, is a fact! To these facts we may add a fact mentioned by Richard Watson together with the inference that he draws from it: "The superstition of antiquity appears to have gone most in favor of baptism by immersion; this is a circumstance which affords a strong presumption that it was one of those additions to the ancient rite which superstition originated." To this judicious remark may be added the fact that superstitious and grossly erroneous sects still go most in favor of plunging. As instances, it is only necessary to refer to the Mormons, Campbellites, and others, who, as is usual with the advocates of plunging, seem to make plunging the one thing needful! And, by the way, this fact itself affords strong reason to suspect that plunging is of superstitious origin, for it has always been the characteristic of the superstitious and grossly erroneous to make their own inventions of more importance than the teachings of God's word. The prominence which Baptists, so called, give to their peculiar dogma is well known. They are proverbial for their proselyting proclivities. And the inducement which they invariably hold out to those whom they would proselyte from other churches is, that they will plunge them, or, as they prefer to express it, immerse them, taking care to assure them that short of this there is no baptism, and, consequently, no admission to the Christian Church, no right to the Sacrament of the Supper, and, in short, that they must remain, if not immersed, "aliens from the commonwealth of Israel, and strangers from the covenants of promise, having no hope, and without God in the world." I have often wondered why there was such a remarkable uniformity among Baptists with regard to these two things, viz.: laying great stress upon being plunged, and making mighty efforts to proselyte from other churches; but I now see that the reason is obviously this, viz.: Most of those who join that church are led to do so by the teaching here specified, and, consequently, believe that plunging, and plunging only, is baptism; and for this reason they recognize all others, all who have not been plunged, as being excluded from the commonwealth of Israel, as stated above. And now being in the Church, and constantly under the same teaching, the original impression becomes more and more deep, and they, of course, become more and more bigoted and exclusive, and looking upon all outside of their Church as being in the deplorable condition of unbaptized heathen, they soon become zealously engaged in the work of proselyting, and to obtain proselytes they hold out the same inducements that had been held out to themselves, and that had proved successful. Hence it is that Anabaptists are so unanimous in this particular, especially in connection with a revival which may be progressing in a given locality: then immersion is their alpha and their omega; and consequently, those who join them do so, in most intances, on this single consideration. Thus it is that *plunging* and *proselyting* go together! This attempt to account for the proselyting proclivities of the Anabaptists, and for their zeal and unanimity in this regard, is really the best apology we can make for them; for if they believe that those whom they proselyte, or attempt to proselyte, from other churches, are really in the covenant of grace and in the fold of Christ, their proselyting practices deserve much severe censure.

But, however we may apologize for the proselyting

practice of the Anabaptists, it must still appear to be a very serious matter when it is remembered that they cause all whom they proselyte from other churches to renounce their previous baptism, as being no baptism, and, consequently, to recognize and declare their plunging to be the only baptism! Now, it is not possible, on calm reflection, to view this as being a matter of little or no importance. Just look at it again. Here are those who say that God, for Christ's sake has pardoned their sins, that he has given them the Spirit of adoption whereby we cry " Abba, Father." That Spirit now bears witness with their spirits that they are the children of God; they were baptized, say, by their spiritual father, who has grown old and gray-headed in the service of his Master, and whose labors by the Divine blessing have been instrumental in the salvation of multitudes; and by him these persons have been received to the communion of saints, amongst whom they have lived, we may suppose, for several years, rejoicing in hope of the glory of God; and being fed with the bread of life by that same spiritual father, and being helped on their way by those with whom they first united, they are still going on their way rejoicing. Now let us suppose that one of these Anabaptists comes along and artfully persuades some of these, perhaps inexperienced and unsuspecting, that they never received Christian baptism, that they must follow Christ down into the water, that they must be buried with him in baptism, that Philip and the Eunuch went down into the water and came up out of the water. And after mixing up all these terms so as to convey the idea that they all mean immersion, for he will not use the word plunge, though he means it, he sums up by assuring those unsuspecting and inexperienced ones that sprinkling is a modern invention, an invention of popery, that immersion was the only mode practised for more than fifteen hundred years! Finally, in short, he persuades them to renounce their former baptism, as not being Christian baptism, and leads them down to the river and plunges them under the water. The work is now complete; with their former baptism they have been persuaded to renounce their former Church as not being a Christian Church, and those nitherto recognized and loved as Christian brethren and sisters, are recognized and loved as such no longer; they will no longer with them surround the Lord's table, as they had been wont to do, nor will they allow them to come and surround the table that is spread in their new home; nor will they sit at the Sacramental table with the venerable man whom they long loved as their spiritual father, or if they would, those who have proselyted them will not allow them, nor will they allow him to come and partake with them; already there is fixed between them a great gulph! These are facts, and with such facts I could fill many pages, and it was the repetition of such facts, of late, that led me to preach and write as I have now done. I say the *repetition*, for with such doings as these I have often been pained and grieved for many years; and I am sure that my experience in this particular is not much different from that of other ministers who have labored where the Anabaptists had a Church. It was thus that their fathers commenced their operations in the days of Martin Luther, as we shall by and by show, and their children but too faithfully copy fater their example.

Now, whether we believe that the baptism thus renounced was, or was not, Christian baptism, the case is a very serious one. If it was not, then all ministers except those of the Anabaptist persuasion are leading the people astray, and both themselves and their people are unbaptized, as were the countless millions of ministers and members who have lived and died in other than the Anabaptist denomination in past ages; and all this notwithstanding the great learning, great knowledge, thorough investigations, marvellous researches, deep piety, and unquestioned holiness, of multitudes of them; yes, notwithstanding all this, we must conclude, if these proselyting Anabaptists be correct, that they all died ignorant and destitute of Christian baptism! And it was reserved for such men as the ignorant and fanatical John Matthias, a baker of Haerlem, and John Boccold, a journeyman tailor of Leyden, in Germany, to obtain a knowledge of Christian baptism, while the learned and studious Melanchthon, and the great reformer, Luther, were left to live and die alike ignorant and destitute of it! But if all this be too monstrous to be believed, then we are forced to the startling conclusion that these proselyting rebaptizers renounce Christian baptism, declaring it to be no baptism, and lead others, especially the inexperienced and unsuspecting youth who have recently been both converted and baptized, to do the same, simply because they were baptized by sprinkling or pouring; and this is done in defiance of the facts, the indisputable facts, that God instituted sprinkling and pouring, that he calls sprinkling and pouring baptism, and that he himself has invariably baptized by pouring, never by plunging; and, finally, that no man living can refer us to a single text of scripture to show that God ever appointed or practised plunging.

We have already specified the chapters and verses where all these facts, except the last, are asserted by some of the plainest and most unmistakable utterances that have ever reached us from the lips of the Most High! And the last is the fact that he has not appointed or practised *plunging* as the mode of baptism, at least that no man can show us where he has done so. If any can refer us to the chapter and verse, let them do so, and if they do, we will give up this fact, but even then all the other facts will remain! It is evident, then, that the practice of the re-baptizers is serious, awfully serious. God pardons, regenerates, adopts, and baptizes precious souls, and they pronounce that baptism no baptism, and cause the parties thus baptized to do the same thing. God seals his children with the seal of the Christian covenant, and they efface, or attempt, to efface that seal and pronounce it no seal. And for that baptism they substitute plunging, and for that plunging, as the mode of baptism, they cannot produce one clear text from God's word, while, at the same time, it is a positive fact, if the Bible be true, that God both teaches and practises baptism by sprinkling and pouring. I say this is serious, awfully serious. And I give it as my solemn conviction that when these re-baptizers approach any church to pronounce its members unbaptized and to persuade them to renounce their baptism, leave their church, be plunged and join the church of the re-baptizers, they should be rebuked and repelled with all diligence and by the use of every proper means. I believe it is the bounden duty of God's watchmen to do so; and they are recreant to their trust if they permit the re-baptizers or any others to come in and unsettle, pervert, and lead away their young converts and others who, in consequence of inexperience and limited knowledge in some things, are liable to be led astray by designing men, whose object is to build up their own organization, and thus, as Paul expresses it, "*make a gain of them;*" or, as Jude expresses it, "having men's persons in admiration because of advantage." This, we are confident, is the object of many of these proselyting teachers, while many of their members, it is hoped, are simply guided by a mistaken zeal. But whatever may be the motives of these proselyters, it is unquestionably the duty of the Christian shepherd to watch over the flock committed to his care, and not allow these proselyters to steal away his sheep. If, however, the Anabaptists honestly believe that there is no baptism, no entrance to the Christian church but by plunging, and no church but that which is composed of those who have been baptized by plunging, let them go out into the world and convert sinners, and then let them plunge, dip, or immerse them; any way, so that they bring them to heaven; but let them not undertake to pervert and steal the members of other churches by telling them that such churches are not Christian churches, and that their baptism is not Christian baptism—let them not do this. Neither let them, as they often do, especially at the time of a revival, cry out for union with us while they thus believe and teach concerning us. We really believe that union is *an impossibility* while they thus believe and teach, nor can they blame us for questioning their sincerity when they cry for union under such circumstances. And I here give due notice to all whom it may concern, that I will, God being my helper, promptly drive from the fold, of which I am the appointed shepherd, all who may approach it for the purpose of stealing the sheep under my care; nor will I, in future, allow the too-often deceptive and hypocritical cry of union to prevent my doing so. And I shall consider it my special duty to look after those who may be converted by our own labors; these are emphatically our children, and we may not allow them to be stolen from us. I have in the past, for the sake of peace, been more tolerant with proselyters than I mean to be in the future. I feel a good deal like the honest Quaker of whom it is said, that he held to his principle of non-resistance till the pirates were boarding his ship, then he seized his cutlass and began to chop off their hands, exclaiming, "Keep thou thine and we'll keep ours!" That's my principle exactly. And I wish all to understand it. And I think that is the proper way to have union. And those who would not have their hand cut off must give over their piratical practices and keep on board their own ship!

Finally, I take it, that where full and explicit directions are not given in the New Testament with regard to the observance of any ordinance clearly of Divine appointment, such directions are to be sought for in the Old Testament; and if we there find clear and explicit directions given by the Almighty and practised by the Old Testament church, these are obviously the directions to be followed; and we are not at liberty to give directions of our own invention as a substitute for them, simply because they were not formally repeated in the New Testament. Now, it is a fact, as we have already shown, that full and explicit directions are given in the Old Testament to use water by pouring or sprinkling as a sign of the baptism of the Spirit, and also as a sign of moral cleansing by the blood of Jesus; and as we know that baptism is a sign of both these, we are bound to follow these Old Testament directions, especially as the prophets had already apprized us that Jesus would "sprinkle many nations," and as we know that he actually and invariably baptizes by pouring, and also that he *sprinkles the hearts of his people from an evil conscience.* See Heb. x. 22. While furnished with such precept and example, so full and clear, I really think that we are not at liberty to invent a new method; much less are we at liberty to invent a method that is utterly without precedent and that cannot be used either as a sign or as a seal; nor do I think that we are at liberty to leave each one to choose a method of his own, simply because the method Divinely appointed and practised under the Old Testament dispensation is not *formally* re-enacted under the New! To carry out this rule would be utterly disastrous to the Christian system. Of the truth of this statement any one will be convinced by a little reflection. For instance, by this rule we would do away with the Christian sabbath, we would exclude females from the holy sacrament, we would do away with family worship, and, in short, as we have already said, to carry out this rule would be utterly ruinous to the Christian system; but if we follow the common sense rule, to observe and do all that the Lord our God has commanded, and never abrogated, all will be well. But if I should do away with God's method of applying the sign and seal, certainly plunging is the last method I should think of, for the idea of plunging for sealing is absurd in the last degree, nor is there anything in the Christian religion of which it is a sign!

And, though I admit that many human inventions were connected with Christian baptism, even at an early period, I do not admit that baptism proper was utterly done away with; on the contrary, it was retained, and, like many other things of Divine appointment, it seemed extremely difficult to get rid of it. Like truth, it lived in the very rubbish of error; for, after passing through their various washings and other inventions, the finale was baptism proper by effusion. Of the truth of this observation, Taylor, in his Facts and Evidences, gives us very convincing proof. This scholarly and laborious investigator of this subject has presented us with twelve facsimiles of pictorial representations of the mode of baptism as administered by the ancients. In the course of his investigations and researches he found them in ancient churches and other places in the East. They are the work of Grecian and Roman artists, and unmistakably represent the practice of the times to which they belong; and every one of them represents the final act, baptism proper, as being administered by effusion. Some of them profess to represent the baptism of our blessed Lord by John; one professes to represent the baptism of the Emperor, or Constantine, another represents the baptism of a King and Queen, and others represent the baptism of other persons, some named and others not; but in every instance the water is represented as falling upon the subject. With these representations before us, we can but say with Mr. Taylor: "They are vouchers for the time in which they were executed; and, though we cannot hear the men of that generation *viva voce*, and we dare not put words into their lips, yet we may *see* their testimony and judge of its relevancy to the inquiry that engages our attention!"

But all this avails nothing with certain men; they still cry out as they plunge, "There was no other way practised for more than fifteen hundred years." But they probably know nothing about the editor of Calmet's Dictionary, or about his facts either; and, very likely, they do not desire to know, for assertion answers their purpose much better.

INFANT BAPTISM.

CHAPTER X.

Bitter opposition of Antipedobaptists to Infant Baptism—Grounds of their opposition examined and refuted.

BITTERLY as the Anabaptists are opposed to baptism by sprinkling, or pouring, they are still more opposed to the baptism of children by any mode. To infant baptism they seem to retain the same bitterness that characterized the founders of their church, who, as D'Aubigne tells us, said, "Baptism is the baptism of a dog; there is no more use in baptizing an infant than in baptizing a cat." While in other particulars they differ very much and very honorably, from their ignorant and fanatical fathers, in this, we must say, they but too nearly resemble them: it is well known that they usually speak of the baptism of infants with contempt and bitterness; indeed they do not call it baptism at all, but "infant sprinkling." Though the child is consecrated to the adorable Trinity in the most solemn manner, by God's minister, in the use of the most appropriate and impressive ceremony, and accompanied by the most devout prayers of the whole church as they bow before the Lord in his house; yet all this is treated with contempt. And, although they do not use the coarse language of their fathers, as quoted above, yet the best they can do is to pronounce it "infant sprinkling," that is all it amounts to! Though the minister, the believing parents, and the church consecrated the child to the adorable Trinity, Father, Son, and Holy Ghost, applying the seal of the covenant, and offering up the most devout prayers, still these sapient ones can see no more religion in it than they can see in the act of the servant-maid when she applies water to the child's face before dressing it; in either case it is only infant sprinkling; that is all!

But what reason do they assign for all this? What do they offer in justification hereof? Certainly nothing short of very serious and weighty considerations will justify this, if anything will. Do they claim that God has positively forbidden the baptism of children? That he has positively commanded, saying, "Thou shalt not baptize thy children at all?" No, they claim nothing of the sort; no one, however extravagant, ever claimed that there was any such command in God's book. What then? Do they claim that this solemn consecration corrupts the children, and makes them more wicked than the children that are not baptized? No, I think no one claims this. Why, then, are they so bitterly opposed to infant baptism? What reason or reasons do they offer as a justification of their bitter opposition and contempt of infant baptism? They shall speak for themselves. We believe the sum of all their reasons are the following:

They say the command is to baptize those who believe; but the child cannot believe, ergo, the child should not be baptized! In support of this strange reasoning they quote the following texts. Acts viii. 36, 37. The Eunuch said, "What doth hinder me to be baptized?" And

Philip said, "If thou believest with all thy heart, thou mayest." Mark xvi. 16. "He that believeth and is baptized shall be saved, and he that believeth not shall be damned." Here it is assumed that what God says to, or of an adult, applies equally to an infant! Really it is difficult to conceive of an assumption more absurd than this. There are so many things wrong here, that one hardly knows where to commence to point them out. It is assumed that God makes no discrimination between an infant and an adult; that the provisions of the atonement are offered to the adult and to the infant upon the same terms; that all God says to the adult race of mankind, applies equally to infants; that you must not limit one jot or tittle of all he says to the adult race of mankind unless he distinctly tells you to do so! Can anything exceed this in extravagance and unreasonableness? In this way you would first starve to death, and then damn all children, and prove conclusively that God had so appointed; for he says, "if any will not work neither should he eat;" and he also says, "he that believeth not shall be damned." But infants can neither work nor believe, therefore they must first be starved to death and then damned! Now this is precisely the reasoning by which infants are excluded from the right of baptism: in each case the conclusion is reached by assuming that infants are included, where adults only are intended! In this way precisely, it was, that the ancient sect of heretics called Hieraxites, concluded that all children dying in childhood would be damned, for they considered knowledge the procuring cause of salvation, and essential to it; and as infants had not, and could not have knowledge, they concluded they could not be saved! And they could establish their position just as satisfactorily as the Anabaptists establish theirs, for Paul says, "Faith cometh by hearing, and hearing by the word of God." But infants are obviously incapable of hearing and knowing the teachings of God's word, and consequently incapable of faith; and Jesus says, He that believeth not shall be damned. Hence the same conclusion is reached, children cannot be saved. Moreover Jesus has said, "this is life eternal, to know thee, the only true God, and Jesus Christ whom thou hast sent." But children cannot have this knowledge, therefore they cannot have "life eternal!" Thus the reasoning of the ancient Hieraxites, and that of the modern Anabaptists, are exactly the same, and the conclusion the same; only in the one case the damnation of children is asserted, in the other the reasoners do not assert it, though their reasoning being the same implies it; for if the commission given to the disciples proves that infants cannot be baptized, because they cannot believe, it as conclusively proves that they cannot be saved, that they must be damned. Nay, there is more reason for the latter than there is for the former conclusion, for Jesus does not say, he that believeth not shall not be baptized, but he does say, he that believeth not shall be damned. And even if he had said, he that believeth not shall not be baptized, even then it would not follow that infants should not be baptized, for the objects of the threat are obviously those to whom the Gospel should be preached, but the Apostles were not sent out into the world to preach the Gospel to infants, therefore the threat had nothing to do with infants, it neither excluded them from baptism nor from heaven, any more than it excluded from heaven those adults in heathen lands, who never had the chance either to hear a preached gospel, or to be baptized. The argument which Anabaptists deduce, or pretend to deduce from Philip's address to the Eunuch is, of course, based upon the same ridiculous assumption; they assume that what Philip says to the Eunuch equally applies to infants; that all infants are to be saved and baptized upon precisely the same conditions that the Eunuch was; and they would have us address all infants just as Philip addressed the "man of Ethiopia, an Eunuch of great authority under Candace, Queen of the Ethiopians, who had the charge of all her treasure, and had come to Jerusalem to worship." Yes, the assumption is that all infants must be treated precisely as was this great official, and saved and baptized on the very same conditions! Is it not marvellous that any intelligent person should assume and reason in this way? And yet, it is upon this assumption, principally, that the Anabaptists base all their opposition to infant baptism; they are ever and anon quoting these texts to prove that infants should not be baptized because they cannot believe. And why? Because, forsooth, Philip said to the Eunuch, "If thou believest with all thy heart, thou mayest be baptized," therefore they would have all ministers of the Gospel deal with infants just as Philip dealt with this great official, the Ethiopian Eunuch, who came to Jerusalem to worship!

Anabaptists say, there is no command in the New Testament to baptize infants, therefore they should not be baptized. This argument, if it may be called an argument, is like all the preceding; it rests upon a mere assumption, which is little, if anything, better than the assumptions already exposed and refuted. The assumption is this; that no command in the Old Testament is binding, or to be observed, unless formally repeated in the New. This assumption, if fully carried out, would be little less disastrous than the preceding. Now, with regard to the commands and teachings of the Old Testament, the question is not, are they repeated in the New? but are they abrogated in the New? If not, of course the obligation to obey, remains unchanged and unabated; and must continue till the law in the given case is abrogated by Him who enacted it. Now every Christian knows, or should know, that the law with regard to children was enacted in the days of Abraham, and its observance made binding upon the Church, and it has been observed by the church of God, without intermission, from then until now; and that law is recorded in the Old Testament, and it is not abrogated in the New! These are the facts in the case, and such facts as defy successful contradiction. Now the law is simply this; that children should be circumcised, even as soon as they were eight days old, and *that* circumcision was the rite of initiation into the Church; it was also the seal of the Covenant; nay, St. Paul tells us that it was the *sign*, and *seal*, of righteousness had previous to the performance of the rite. Now then, here is the fact, the indisputable fact; *that rite* which included all that we have here specified, was, by the command of God, extended to children, even as soon as they were eight days old! But I will be told that baptism does not take the place of circumcision; I answer, I care not a rush, I am not talking about that just now, we will attend to that in due time. What I claim just now is simply this; *at the time that the church was formally organized, the covenant between God and his people was ratified with Abraham, who, with his children, received the seal of that covenant, and this seal was at the same time the sign and seal of* RIGHTEOUSNESS *previously had, and it was also the rite of initiation into the church of God. And all this, by the command of God, was secured to the infant in common with the parent, and this command was never abrogated!* Now, we repeat the statement, and we repeat it with increased emphasis, the question is not whether this command is repeated in the New Testament; the question is, is it abrogated in the New Testament? To this question there is but one answer, and that is NO! We affirm that God has not cancelled this command, nor has he cancelled one jot or tittle of the rights, privileges and blessings which it secures to children; and if the Anabaptists undertake to do so, they do it on their own authority, and at their own risk. Instead, then, of the Anabaptists asking us, where is this command in the New Testament? we ask them where is it abrogated in the New Testament? And till they can point to the positive annulment, or repeal of this law, they are bound to do as we do; and if they still refuse to obey this confessedly unrepealed law of God, they do so at their own risk, and we must recognize them as transgressors of that law; and as attempting to deprive children of rights and blessings secured to them by the blood of the covenant, and by the promise and command of the Most High. We say the *promise* and the *command:* for when God made the covenant with Abraham, and specified the rights and blessings thus secured, he added, "*thee* and thy seed," and on the day of Pentecost this promise was repeated in these words, "the promise is to you and to your children." The practice of attempting to annul or evade a

Divine law that was enacted long ago, simply because it has not been *re-enacted*, is as absurd as it is pernicious. Suppose one should attempt to evade or annul some of the laws of this State or nation, and plead in justification the fact that they were not re-enacted at the last session of the Legislature; would not the very children tell him that re-enactment was not necessary, that every law remained in force, till repealed by the power that enacted it? And this is specially true of the laws of God. Yet the Anabaptists attempt to evade, or annul the law under consideration, simply because it has not been formally re-enacted or repeated in the New Testament! I say *formally*, for it has been repeated, though not with its original formality, for this was not necessary.

CHAPTER XI.

It is shown that Infant Baptism takes the place of Circumcision—Early Christian Fathers are quoted—Testimony of Pelagius—The Antipedobaptist dogma one of the most modern of religious errors—Baxter is quoted—Other Fathers are quoted.

THOUGH it is not at all necessary to the validity of the position here taken to prove that baptism takes the place of circumcision, yet being convinced that it does, I will make a few remarks which I think will satisfy the unprejudiced that it does.

Circumcision and the passover are unquestionably done away with by Him who appointed them. And Baptism and the Lord's Supper are unquestionably appointed by the same authority. The doing away of the former, and the appointment of the latter, took place at the same time, and the disuse of the former, and the use of the latter, have continued in the Christian Church to the present day; and it is not questioned that the supper takes the place of the passover; and, if baptism does not take the place of circumcision, then we have nothing in its place. But the truth is, this is neither more nor less than saying and unsaying, and such saying and unsaying as leave the facts unaltered; for the facts that circumcision was done away with, and baptism introduced at the same time, and by the same authority, remain facts, whatever we may say. And it is both folly and contradiction to say that the one does not take the place of the other: especially when it is remembered and admitted, as it must be, that baptism is what circumcision was, viz.: a sign and seal, and also an initiatory rite. The amount is this, to express it still more briefly: He who appointed circumcision for the purposes here specified, has appointed baptism for the same specified purposes; and the annulment of the one, and the appointment of the other, took place at the same time. Now to admit all this, and yet deny that the one takes the place of the other, is, I maintain, folly and self-contradiction. Folly, because nothing is gained by it, for the facts remain, and they comprehend all we claim, viz.: the rights of children under the present as under the former dispensation. And it is self-contradiction, for that which is denied is the very same that has been admitted by admiting the facts, which must be admitted; and the facts comprehend all we claim. Our claims, therefore, are established with all the certainty of fact, notwithstanding the play upon the words *take the place of*, for the objection is really a play upon these words. It is admitted that the one was removed, and the other appointed, and that the latter answers the purposes of the former, and yet it is denied that the latter takes the place of the former! Nonsense! the fact is, no man would ever have said so had it not appeared to him that the admission would militate against his system.

Water baptism is substituted for circumcision because, while it answers all the purposes of the former, as specified above, it does more. It is more congenial with the more mild dispensation of the Gospel, which is emphatically the dispensation of the spirit. And it is a sign of the baptism of the spirit, as circumcision could not be. Hence, under that dispensation there was divinely appointed sprinkling and pouring in connection with it; while under this dispensation baptism answers all the purposes.

It also does away with the distinction which necessarily existed between male and female while circumcision was in use. The doing away of this distinction, by substituting baptism for circumcision, is very forcibly and beautifully expressed by the apostle Paul in the following words: "For as many of you as have been baptized into Christ, have put on Christ. There is neither Jew nor Greek, there is neither bond nor free, there is neither male nor female: for ye are all one in Christ Jesus." (Gal. iii. 7, 8) To prove that baptism does not take the place of circumcision, certain ignorant persons, and amongst them sometimes females, have urged the fact that while circumcision was not, baptism is, administered to females. To such females we recommend Paul's very sensible and appropriate advice: "Let them ask their husbands at home." And if their husbands are as ignorant as themselves, which is very likely, we can only sympathize with them. Meantime we claim that the words quoted above prove just the reverse of what the objector designs to prove by the fact stated. That baptism takes the place of circumcision is evident from the following Scripture also. Speaking of our completeness in Christ, the apostle says to the Colossians: "In whom also ye are circumcised with the circumcision made without hands, in putting off the body of the sins of the flesh by the circumcision of Christ, buried with him in baptism," &c. (Col. ii. 11, 12.)

Having quoted this text, Mr. Watson observes, having specified other particulars in which baptism takes the place of circumcision: "Here baptism is made the initiatory rite of the new dispensation, that by which the Colossians were joined to Christ *in* whom they are said to be '*complete;*' and so certain is it that baptism has the same office and import now as circumcision formerly, —with this difference only, that the object of faith was then future, and now it is Christ *as come*—that the Apostle expressly calls baptism '*the ci'cumcision of Christ;*' the circumcision instituted by him, which phrase he puts out of the reach of frivolous criticism, by adding exegetically, 'buried with him in *baptism.*' For unless the Apostle here calls baptism 'the circumcision of Christ,' he asserts that we 'put off the body of the sins of the flesh,' that is, become new creatures by virtue of our Lord's own personal circumcision; but if this be absurd, then the only reason for which he can call baptism 'the circumcision of Christ,' or Christian circumcision, is, that it has taken the place of the Abrahamic circumcision, and fulfils the same office of introducing believing men into God's covenant, and entitling them to the enjoyment of spiritual blessings." The phrase, circumcision of Christ, so evidently means Christian baptism, that this close and accurate reasoner does not hesitate to say that Paul himself has "put it out of the reach of frivolous criticism." Doddridge, too, in his notes on the place, takes the same view. Having quoted the words "putting off the body of the sins of the flesh," he adds, "renouncing all the deeds of it. Your engagements to this you have expressed by that ordinance which I may call the circumcision of Christ; it being that by which he hath appointed that we should be initiated into His Church as the members of it." Thus he represents Paul as saying of baptism, "that ordinance which I may call the circumcision of Christ." The propriety of all this will appear still more clear when it is remembered that baptism and circumcision symbolize the same thing, namely, the removal of moral uncleanness; though they do it in different ways, yet both are very significant of this thing. Hence Philo, as quoted by Whitby, says that "circumcision imports the cutting off our sinful pleasures and passions, and our impious opinions." What circumcision represents by *cutting off*, baptism still more forcibly represents by the idea of *washing away*. And Peter, referring both to circumcision and baptism, speaks of them as symbolizing this moral cleansing by "the putting away of the filth of the flesh." Moral impurity is often called *filth*, both in the Old and New Testaments. See, for instance, Isaiah iv. 4, Ezek. xxxii. 25, and Rev. xxii. 11.

After showing, at great length, and by most conclusive evidence, that Christian baptism takes the place of circumcision, Mr. Watson adds: "This argument is sufficiently extended to show that the Antipædobaptist writers have in vain endeavored to prove that baptism has not been appointed in the room of circumcision; a point on which, indeed, they were bound to employ all their strength; for the substitution of baptism for circumcision being established, one of their main objections to infant baptism, as we will just now show, is rendered wholly nugatory." Having adduced the further evidence here promised, he sums up thus: "If then we bring all these considerations under one view, we shall find it sufficiently established that baptism is the sign and seal of the covenant of grace under its perfected dispensation; —that it is the grand initiatory act by which we enter into this covenant, in order to claim all its spiritual blessings, and to take upon ourselves all its obligations:—that it was appointed by Jesus Christ in a manner which plainly put it in the place of circumcision;—that it is now the means by which men become Abraham's spiritual children, and heirs with him of the promise, which was the office of circumcision, until the seed, the Messiah, should come;—and that baptism is therefore expressly called by St. Paul, 'the circumcision of Christ,' or Christian circumcision, in a sense which can only import that baptism has now taken the place of the Abrahamic rite." After refuting another objection of Antipædobaptist writers, stated by Mr. Booth, Mr. Watson concludes thus: "We may here add, that an early father, Justin Martyr, takes the same view of the substitution of circumcision by Christian baptism: "We Gentiles," Justin observes, "have not received that circumcision according to the flesh, but that which is spiritual—and moreover, for indeed we were sinners, we have received this in *baptism*, through God's mercy, and it is enjoined on all to receive it in like manner." According to this father, *circumcision is received in baptism, and it is enjoined upon all!* But this same ancient father is still more distinct in the following quotation, which is handed down to us as containing his words verbatim: "We Gentile Christians are circumcised by baptism with Christ's circumcision;" and in support of this view he quotes Col. ii. 11, 12. He also says, "we were discipled in our childhood." Now when it is remembered that this father was born about A. D. 133, and that he is here defending the practice of the whole Christian Church in opposition to the Jews, who still contended for circumcision, it must be admitted, we think, that this testimony is overwhelmingly conclusive. Not because his testimony or practice, or that of any other man, or number of men, is a rule for us when unsupported by Scripture, but because it is quite sufficient to show what were the facts with regard to the views and the practice of the early Christian Church; so early, that some still living were familiar with some of the apostles, at least with the apostle John, and his teachings: and their views, according to the testimony of this father, were, that baptism took the place of circumcision; and, accordingly, that they "discipled," that is, baptized in "childhood." Turning to Taylor's "Facts and Evidences," I find that writer furnishes the following quotation from this same Justin Martyr: "Why, if circumcision be a good thing, do we not use it as well as the Jews did? The answer is, because we Gentile Christians are circumcised by baptism with Christ's circumcision." Now this shows most conclusively what were the views and practice of the primitive church with regard to baptism. Their views were that Christ gave baptism in the place of circumcision, and that they practised accordingly; for if these were not the views and practice of the primitive church this prominent minister could not write and publish what every Christian then living must have known to be a glaring falsehood. It would not be possible, for instance, for a prominent minister in the Anabaptist church of the present day to publish a treatise in defence of baptism by Sprinkling, and especially in defence of the baptism of infants, asserting that these were the views and practice of the entire church of which he was a minister, and that they did so upon the authority of Christ and his apostles, and that they had always believed and practised thus; I say no such minister could do so while in a sane state; and if he should, of course the whole Anabaptist church would contradict and reject his statement. Let it be acknowledged, then, as we think every intelligent and honest man must acknowledge, that Justin Martyr and other fathers could not write thus if these were not the views and practice of the primitive church; and if these were evidently the views and practice of the primitive church, with what face can Anabaptist ministers tell the masses of the people, who know no better, that the baptism of infants is a modern, a popish invention? The best excuse we can possibly make for such ministers is that they themselves are ignorant; "the blind lead the blind." Mr. Taylor also gives us the following quotation from the writings of John Chrysostom: "There was pain and trouble in the practice of that Jewish circumcision; but our circumcision, I mean the grace of baptism, gives cure without pain; and this for infants as well as men." Here, as late as the latter end of the fourth century, this father still speaks of the "Jewish circumcision" and "our circumcision," and by "our circumcision" he tells us he means *baptism;* and, observe, he is not speaking of *his* views and practice, but of those of the entire Christian Church at that time, as Justin Martyr had done more than two hundred years before.

The incident that is recorded as having occurred at the Council of Carthage is well known. The substance of it is this. One Fedus, not being present at the Council, wrote to the presiding bishop, Cyprian, to know whether a child should be baptized before it was eight days old; to this inquiry Cyprian and the whole Council, consisting of sixty-six bishops, replied that it was not necessary to delay baptism till the eighth day. Now I will simply ask, could an Antipedobaptist minister write thus to a council of sixty-six of his brethren ? and could such a council reply as did that at Carthage ? To these questions there is, of course, but one answer, and that is *No;* such a communication could not be sent to such a body and receive such an answer; and, for the same reason, it was not possible that such a communication could have been sent to the Council at Carthage and receive the reply here recorded, if, as we are told by the Antipedobaptists, the whole Christian Church then believed and practised as they do now ; nor could Fedus have thus written, nor was it possible for the Council to reply as it did, had not the baptism of children been the belief and practice of the primitive church ! What, then, can we think of those who assert, as was publicly asserted here of late, that the practice of the present Anabaptist Church was the only practice " for more than fifteen hundred years ?" We certainly have but too much reason to conclude that such men have learned, and do understand the fact, that bold assertions will answer their purpose better than argument with a certain class !

The fact is, though at a very early period there were many departures from Apostolic teaching and practice, it does not seem to have occurred to the most daring of the inventors of error to deny children the right of baptism. Hence, when Pelagius was charged with this, he seems to have been perfectly shocked, even as much as if he had been charged with murder. Hence he complains thus: "Men slander me as if I denied the Sacrament of Baptism to infants," and having denied the slander with horror, he says, he *never heard even of the most impious heretic* that was guilty of doing so! See Hibbard on Infant Baptism, p. 217. The truth is, the exclusion of infants from Christian Baptism is amongst the most modern of human inventions, as a religious dogma. Hence Baxter says: "I am fully satisfied that you cannot show me any society, I think not one man, that ever objected to infant baptism till about two hundred years ago. I find Christ did once place little children in the Church, and no man breathing can show me one word of Scripture where ever Christ did put them out again." "About two hundred years ago." He refers to the origin of the Anabaptist views by John Matthias and King John of Leyden, and other German fanatics in the days of Luther. Before this time, we do not remember to have read of a single individual who is even charged with excluding infants from baptism, unless it be Pierre de Bruis, in the 12th Century, and the record is very unreliable, for the charge is brought against him by the Abbot Clugny, his deadly enemy. The charge which the Abbot brings against him, is this. The Abbot says: "He," Pierre de Bruis, "denies that children, before they arrive at years of intelligence, can be saved by baptism, or that the faith of another person can be useful to them, since, according to those of his opinion, it is not the faith of another which saves, but the faith of the individual with baptism, according to our Lord's words: 'He that believeth and is baptized shall be saved; but he that believeth not shall be damned!'" From the quotation itself I am strongly inclined to believe that the charge is not truthful; for the wording of the charge conveys to me the idea that the opposition of Bruis was not to the baptism of children, but to the Popish dogma that children are saved by baptism and cannot be saved without it; for the Abbot charges him with denying that children "can be saved by baptism," and he no doubt did deny that children are saved by baptism in the Popish sense; but could we hear him speak for himself we would, no doubt, hear him deny the other part of the charge as Pelagius did, for he was a good man, and was burned for his adherence to the truth, in 1126. It is probably to this man that Baxter refers when he says: "I think not one man." The case of Pierre de Bruis, as here referred to, may be found in the History of the Vaudois, by Antoine Monastier.

In addition to the quotations already given from the fathers, we will add the following, which we find in our memoranda but cannot say what we quoted from; they are, however, faithful quotations, which we made in the course of our reading. Irenæus speaks of the baptism of "infants, little ones, and children." He flourished about A. D. 178, and was acquainted with Polycarp, who was a disciple of the Apostle John. Origen refers to infant baptism in proof of original sin, and says the Church baptized infants "because the Apostles commanded it." He flourished in the third century. Ambrose, too, refers to the baptism of infants in proof of original sin, and says "it was practised in the Apostles' times." He wrote in the fourth century. Augustine, too, makes a similar statement for the same purpose, and says of infant baptism that "it was practised in the Apostles' time." He wrote in the fifth century. In defence of the same doctrine, Chrysostom says: "For this reason we baptize infants also." He wrote in the fourth century. Tertullian, we are told, advised the delay of infant baptism, but this whim resulted from another error which he had embraced, viz.: that they were saved by baptism, and that, consequently, if any one died after baptism, before committing sin, such an one was saved; but errorist as he was, he was no Antipedobaptist. To these testimonies we may add the fact that the Greek Church does, and always did, baptize infants. Speaking of Tertullian, Mr. Watson says, vol ii. p. 645: "So little, indeed, were Tertullian's absurdities regarded, that he appears to have been quite forgotton by this time, for Augustine says he never heard of any Christian, Catholic or Sectary, who taught any other doctrine than that infants are to be baptized."—De Pecc. Mor. Cap. 6.

CHAPTER XII.

It is shown that Infant Baptism has been practised from Apostolic times—Not One clear case of Opposition to Infant Baptism till the Sixteenth Century—Appealing to, and Reasoning with, the Antipedobaptists—Astounding Facts Stated—They cannot tell us when the Practice of Baptizing Infants Commenced—We can tell them When and by Whom Opposition thereto Commenced—Infant Baptism the Uncontradicted Practice of the Church from Apostolic till Modern Times.

Now, in view of this overwhelming array of testimony, and we could add much more, we will indulge in a few brief reflections to which we invite the serious attention of all, whether Pedobaptist or Antipedobaptist. And, first, observe, we do not produce the teaching and example of either the ancients or the moderns to prove that children should be baptized; though teaching and practice so uniform are not to be disregarded even as proof, nevertheless, for our authority and proof we rely upon the word of God. But we produce all this array of testimony and practice to prove *that infant baptism is no innovation, that it has been practised from Apostolic times to the present time, as circumcision was in all the previous ages of the Church!* As late as the fifth century, Augustine and Pelagius, who were opposed in other things, give their testimony to this fact, that they never heard of one, no not the most impious heretic, who opposed infant baptism, or taught any other doctrine; and Baxter asserts that he never heard of a society, he thinks not a single individual, who opposed infant baptism till about two hundred years before his time, that is, till the sixteenth century! What an astounding fact! For a period of some fifteen hundred years, dating from Apostolic times, not a single clear case of opposition to infant baptism in all Christendom; though during that period the devil and errorists seem to have introduced every imaginable error save that of the Antipedobaptists; for some reason they did not dare to introduce this error till the sixteenth century from the Christian era; surely this is one of the most wonderful facts of history! We may safely say, I think, that during this period every other doctrine of the Christian system was assailed, in one way or other, but it remained for the crazy, lawless, German fanatics of the sixteenth century to attack the doctrine, the Christian doctrine, of infant baptism, and found an Antipedobaptist Church!

To the Antipedobaptists we say, "Come now and let us reason together;" do not get vexed with our statement of facts, or with our reflections upon these facts; we are honest, we are sincere, we believe what we say, we are searching after the truth as well as the facts in the case, and if we know ourselves we are prepared to receive the truth wherever we find it. If, as you say, infant baptism is an innovation, a novelty, a human invention, will you please tell us when and where this novelty, this human invention, was introduced, and by whom? Or if you cannot tell us the time when, and the persons by whom, it was introduced, will you be good enough to point us to a period since the Christian era, when it was not practised? We cannot find such a period, Baxter could not find such a period, nor could he point to a single society that ever opposed the doctrine till the period specified; nor could any of the Christian Fathers point to such a party in their time, or "in the old time before them," nor could they point us to a period since the Christian era when infant baptism was not practised. Many others, too, very many, of the learned and wise have searched with great care and perseverance, but they have all failed, utterly failed, to discover a period since the Christian era when infant baptism was not practised in the Christian Church. Now, if the Antipedobaptists have discovered what all others have failed to discover, will they be good enough to favor us with the discovery? Will they tell us at what period since the Apostolic times infant baptism was introduced into the Christian Church? As honest men they are bound to do this, or never again call it a novelty, an innovation. If it is an innovation, how is it that, unlike all other innovations, its introduction called forth no opposition or discussion? It is a fact that children were received into the Church by the divinely appointed initiatory rite from the days of Abraham till the days of the Apostles. Now, is it possible that a divine appointment of so long standing, of such vital importance, and so wide in its application as to embrace all the children of all the worshippers of the true God, could be abrogated and no one know when the abrogation took place? Is it possible that all the children of all the worshippers of the true God could be at once excluded from the Church of God without opposition or complaint from either Jew or Gentile? Or, if there was complaint or opposition, is it possible that all the facts in the case could have been excluded from history, so completely excluded that we do not find in any of the Church Councils the record of one jot or tittle of complaint, opposition, or even discussion with regard to the exclusion of children from their long and divinely-appointed place in the Church of God? Is it possible that believing parents could be all at once so divested of all natural and religious feeling that they could submit to have their children excluded from the Covenant and Church of God without offering any resistance, objection, or even complaint? Is it possible that the Jews, whose children under the former dispensation had been received into the Church, received into covenant relation to God, and had received the sign and seal of the covenant, is it possible, I say, that these Jews could all at once submit to the annulment, the reversion, of all this without opposition or complaint, especially as no one produced, or pretended to produce, a jot or tittle of Divine authority for this serious change in the Divine constitution? Is it possible that the unbelieving Jews, the deadly enemies of the new dispensation, who sought every occasion to object to, and depreciate the Christian system, could fail to notice a change which afforded such just ground for objection and opposition? Or if they did object and oppose, is it possible that history could be entirely silent with regard to these facts? Is it possible that neither Jew nor Gentile, inspired or uninspired, believing or unbelieving, should ever record one jot or tittle with regard to the change, or the opposition thereto, if such change and opposition had taken place? Now, in answer to all these questions we do not hesitate to reply, No; such a change could not take place without opposition, complaint, or discussion; much less could it take place without any one knowing when, how, or by whom it was made. We therefore conclude that *the change did not take place ; we must so* conclude, for the contrary conclusion would be in favor of what we claim to be impossible !

The Antipedobaptists have not to ask us when, how, and by whom their dogma was introduced ; we tell them without being asked. We tell them the time when, the place where, and the parties by whom their antiscriptural dogma was introduced. We tell them the opposition that its introduction met with, and who they were who made the opposition to it; even Luther, Melancthon, Calvin, and, in short, the entire Christian world, with the exception of the few lawless fanatics who introduced it, and who were the cause of much disgrace and injury to the great reformation. And we refer them to the pages of history, where they may find the facts recorded ! And we challenge them to show us, to tell us when, where and by whom their antiscriptural novelty was introduced before this time : and we claim that their inability to do so, makes our argument as complete as argument can be ! . Wall says that Peter Bruis, about 1130, was the first Antipedobaptist teacher who had a regular congregation. (Hist., part 2, c. 7.) Even if this were admitted it would not help the matter, it only shows that Antipedobaptism is an innovation of comparatively modern introduction. But we have already shown that there is no evidence that this man ever opposed infant baptism as being unscriptural. Bishop Tomlin says that the Anabaptists of Germany took their rise in the beginning of the 16th century ; but it does not appear that there was any congregation of Anabaptists in England till the year 1640. This is without doubt the origin of the present Antipedobaptist church, as we have already shown. If they had an existence before then, let them show us when and where!

Closing his arguments in favor of infant baptism, Mr. Watson says: "That a practice which can be traced up to the very first periods of the church, and has been till within very modern times, its uncontradicted practice, should have a lower authority than apostolic usage and appointment, may be pronounced impossible. It is not like one of those trifling, though somewhat superstitious, additions which even in early times began to be made to the sacraments; on the contrary, it involves a principle so important as to alter the very nature of the sacrament itself." Inst., vol. ii., p. 646. Mark these two statements in this quotation; till within very modern times infant baptism was the *uncontradicted* practice of the church. Second; the Antipedobaptist dogma involves a principle so important as to *alter the very nature of the sacrament itself!* Let it be borne in mind, then, that this Antipedobaptist dogma is not only a novelty, but a very serious error, as we shall show more fully pretty soon.

CHAPTER XIII.

The objection that Infant Baptism is incompatible with Man's Natural Rights is shown to be ridiculous—It contains the very germ of Infidelity, and even Atheism—Objection that Circumcision was a Civil Contract is refuted—Many absurdities exposed.

FINALLY, lest all the other objections to infant baptism should prove insufficient, Antipedobaptists tell us that it is incompatible with man's natural rights; that baptism should be delayed till the child is capable of choosing for itself! This objection is not only ridiculous, but it contains the very *germ* of infidelity. The late Robert Owen, the founder of that form of infidelity called Socialism, took the same ground, and insisted that all religious instruction should be delayed till the child is at least thirteen years old! Truly the devil spoke like himself when he made this proposal! I say this objection contains the very *germ* of infidelity, for it is in direct opposition to *well-known Bible teaching;* seeing that book informs us that God commanded the child to be consecrated to himself, and the seal of the covenant applied as early as eight days after the child is born. It is clear, then, that the issue is joined, not with us, but with Bible teaching, known, unmistakable Bible teaching! And, as we before showed, it will not mend the matter to say that baptism does not take the place of circumcision, for the facts are not altered at all; if baptism is incompatible with man's natural rights so was circumcision, seeing it laid the child under as much obligation as does baptism. Nor will it do for the Anabaptists to say, as they have said, that circumcision was a civil contract, and that the obligations and blessings involved were of a temporal character; for surely it is not a greater interference with the child's natural rights to lay it under obligation to serve Almighty God than it is to lay it under obligations of a civil or national character. But the fact is, this objection of the Antipedobaptists only serves to show the desperateness of their case; for the moral character of the Abrahamic covenant, of which circumcision was the seal, is unmistakably taught both in the Old and New Testaments, as the following texts do most clearly show. Jer. iv. 4: "Circumcise yourselves to the Lord, and take away the foreskins of your heart, ye men of Judah and inhabitants of Jerusalem." Deut. xxx. 6: "And the Lord thy God will circumcise thine heart and the heart of thy seed, to love the Lord thy God with all thine heart, and with all thy soul, that thou mayest live." Deut. x. 15, 16: "Only the Lord had a delight in thy fathers to love them, and he chose their seed after them, even you above all people, as it is this day. Circumcise, therefore, the foreskin of your heart, and be no more stiffnecked." Romans ii. 28: "For he is not a Jew which is one outwardly in the flesh; but he is a Jew which is one inwardly; and circumcision is that of the heart, in the spirit, and not in the letter, whose praise is not of men, but of God." St. Paul says, "Abraham received the sign of circumcision, a seal of the righteousness of the faith which he had, yet being uncircumcised." A careful study of these and similar texts, which abound in the Old and New Testaments, will satisfy any one that circumcision was the seal of the covenant of grace, and a seal of righteousness, or justification, previously had, and that it was also a sign of moral purity, or sanctification; this was signified by the removal, or "putting away" of "the filth of the flesh;" it was also a sign or badge of the peculiar relation which the circumcised party sustained to God. Now, with such teachings as these before us, I think it is not saying too much to say that it must be a bad cause which forces its advocates to say that circumcision was merely a civil transaction, and that it only involved temporal blessings and obligations. And its badness becomes still more apparent, when it forces its advocates to say that such a transaction is incompatible with man's natural rights! for that is a declared opposition to the teachings of God's word, and is, therefore, infidel in its principle, as we before said.

This objection not only contains the germ of infidelity, but it contains the germ of atheism; for it assumes it to be the natural right of the child to choose whether he shall or shall not be consecrated to God Almighty; whether he shall or shall not acknowledge his obligations to, and serve God Almighty. This objection assumes it to be an open question whether the God who created and redeemed has a right to put forth such claims, and that all these questions are to be left undecided till the child is of age to choose and decide for itself; that its judgment and authority in the case are superior to those of the Almighty; and that the Almighty has no right or authority to decide in the case till he first consults the child after it is capable of judging in the case and obtains its consent! It assumes, too, that revelation and man's natural rights are at variance, that the former is subversive of the latter, and, therefore, unjust and should not be submitted to! It assumes—what does it assume? In a word, everything that is wrong, and nothing that is right. And yet we have listened to, and even countenanced, this *antipedo*, this *infidel*, this *atheistical* objection, till both parents and children in our very churches have learned to utter it in justification of their opposition, their daring opposition, to the plain teachings of God's word!

But the absurd, as well as the infidel and atheistical, character of this objection deserves specification. If in deference to the natural rights of children we may not consecrate them to God, may not receive them into the church, into the covenant of grace, and apply to them the seal of that covenant; may not lay them under obligation to serve God when they come to the years of understanding, what may we do? On the same principle I do not see why we should not leave them to choose what teacher they shall have, what school they shall go to, what kind of instruction they shall have, or whether they shall have any instruction at all! And if we do, I am strongly inclined to believe that they will choose the latter; and if they should, I do not see what right we have to oppose their choice any more than we had a right to choose for them before they were capable of making a choice! Nor do I see what right we have, on this principle, to choose anything for the child, not even the kind of dress it shall wear, or whether it shall wear any dress at all! And the probability is that it would not, if left to its own choice! In all likelihood, if left to itself, it would, if it should live, be alike destitute of *learning*, *clothing* and *religion!* Such, doubtless, would be the result of this Antipedo-baptist objection if fully carried out. And after experimentizing thus upon it for a few years, we would, doubtless, have a better knowledge of it than we have now; but the knowledge would be very dearly bought! As it is never wise to experimentize upon error; let us rather abide by the good old way, and experimentize upon the truth, even the truth enjoined upon us in the following scriptures: "Ye stand this day all of you before the Lord your God; your captains of your tribes, your elders and your officers, with all the men of Israel, your LITTLE ONES, your wives, and thy stranger that is in thy camp, from the hewer of thy wood, unto the drawer of thy water: that thou shouldest ENTER INTO COVENANT with the LORD thy God, AND INTO THE OATH, which the LORD thy God maketh with thee this day." And now that your *little ones* as well as yourselves sustain a covenant relation to God, see that you consult *not their choice*, but the word of your covenant God, and teach them to "observe and do all his commandments." "And these words which I command thee this day shall be in thine heart; and thou shalt teach them diligently unto thy children, and shalt talk of them when thou sittest in thine house, and when thou walkest by the way, and when thou liest down, and when thou risest up." Thus, "train up a child in the way he should go, and when he is old he will not depart from it." Here you have God's *command* and God's *promise;* keep them as did Abraham, of whom the LORD hath said, "I know him, that he will command his children and his household after him, and they shall keep the way of the Lord, to do justice and judgment." Rest assured of it, that it will be much wiser to do this than to leave your children "to choose for themselves." If, in reply to all this, the Anabaptist should say: "But we do teach our children;" then, my reply is, never more tell us to leave *our* children "to choose for themselves." Nor are you at liberty to choose for yourself, even as to what you shall or shall not teach; you are bound both "to *teach* and *do* all that the LORD thy God hath commanded thee." And he hath taught thee to consecrate thy children, as well as thyself, to him in holy baptism; as we shall now show by proof drawn more directly from his own word.

CHAPTER XIV.

Direct Scripture proof—Infants have the necessary qualifications for baptism—Their claim more clear than that of any adult—Romans, v. 12, 18, 19, explained—The infant has the same qualifications for baptism, that Abraham had for circumcision; the same that believing adults have for baptism—A close connection between Infant Baptism and Infant Salvation on the one hand, and between Antipedobaptism and infant damnation on the other—Remarks on the moral nature of infants.

WE will now defend infant baptism by a direct appeal to the word of God. And in doing this we purpose to show that the infant derives its *right* to baptism, not from its parents or from the Church, but from Jesus Christ, through whose atonement it has also a *qualification* for baptism, and that qualification is *justification;* and both the *right* to, and *qualification* for, baptism, it has *unconditionally.* And both the right to, and qualification, for, baptism being unconditional, it will follow, of course, that, if any one infant has the right and the qualification, all infants have; unless it can be shown that Jesus did not die for all; and this cannot be shown till it is first shown that the following and similar declarations contain a falsehood. "One died for all." "He, by the grace of God, tasted death for every man." Now, we take the ground that what is thus secured to infants, cannot be taken from them by the whims and fancies of men, nor yet by the enactments of Synods and Councils, True, men may deprive infants of baptism as they may deprive them of food, but their right thereto remains *unalienated* and *inalienable!*

Having thus stated our position and purpose, we now proceed to the proof.

The first Scripture we quote is from the fifth chapter of the Epistle to the Romans. We quote verses 12, 18, and 19 together, because they are evidently connected, the intervening verses being parenthetical. "Wherefore, as by one man sin entered into the world, and death by sin; and so death passed upon all men, for that all have sinned. Therefore, as by the offence of one judgment came upon all men to condemnation, even so by the righteousness of one, the free gift came upon all men unto justification of life. For as by one man's disobedience many were made sinners, so by the obedience of one shall many be made righteous."

Let us now carefully notice what it is that Paul says "came upon all men," and how it came. And, observe, we have nothing to do just here with what came, or may come, upon any individual by his own individual acts; we have only to do with what "came upon all," "by one."

Here are the specifications; some of them are quoted from the parenthetical verses, they being explanatory of the verses which we have quoted above:

"By one man sin entered into the world." "Judgment came upon all men." That is, the sentence of the judge, or, as we sometimes say, the sentence of a broken law; and that sentence is specifically declared to be "condemnation," "death."

We now enquire how was all this brought, or caused by one? The answer is, "by one that sinned;" "by one man's offence ; " " by one man's disobedience ;" by " Adam's transgression."

So much " came upon all men," in the way here specified. So far there can be no mistake, for we have Paul's declaration for every particular. Of course the judgment, or sentence, was not fully executed upon our first parents, in consequence of the gracious interposition of our Saviour. If it had been, it would have extended to their unborn posterity, resulting in the *non-existence* thereof ; so that the entire posterity of the guilty pair owe their very existence to Jesus ! But we are anticipating the next question.

Having seen what it is that " came upon all by one," even by Adam ; let us now see what it is that " came upon all men" by *one*, even by Christ.

Here, too, let it be distinctly noticed, we have nothing to do with what came, or may come, upon any individual conditionally, for what is here specified " came " before those to whom it " came " were capable of performing a condition : this is not only stated by the Apostle at different times, especially in this chapter, and more especially in the verses quoted above, but it is implied in the very specifications themselves. The specifications are these. " The grace of God ;" " the free gift ;" "the gift of grace." And all this " came upon all unto justification of life." The " judgment " which " came upon all " was " unto condemnation," and the " free gift " which " came upon all " was " unto justification of life." In the one case " condemnation " came, and life was forfeited ; in the other " justification " came, and life was restored ; and all this, in each case, so far as Adam's posterity was concerned, without their own personal act : the " condemna-

tion," came through Adam, the "justification " through Christ.

But how did this " grace of God," and this "gift of grace," come " upon all ?" The Apostle tells us in the following words: "*By the righteousness of* ONE;" "*by the obedience of* ONE." The results of Adam's sin, to his *infant* posterity, are removed by Christ's righteousness; the results of Adam's " disobedience," to his *infant* posterity are removed by the "obedience" of Christ, who "became obedient unto death, even the death of the cross." Thus the great REDEEMER, the RESTORER, has fairly met the *results* of Adam's " offence," so far as his *unacting* posterity are concerned, and it is of them that we are now speaking. The " condemnation" that came upon Adam's posterity, by Adam's disobedience without their own act, is removed by the "justification" that came through Christ's righteousness, without their own act. So that every infant sustains a justified relation to God, through Christ's atonement, *and this is its qualification for baptism;* and this same justification is that which qualifies adult believers for baptism; and it was justification that qualified Abraham for circumcision; and all this Paul asserts and proves in the Scripture before us. In the last verse of the fourth chapter, he says Christ " was delivered for our offences, and was raised again for our δικαιωσιν, justification; and in the eighteenth verse of the following chapter, when speaking of what " came upon all " through the sin of Adam, and the righteousness of Christ, he says, " by the righteousness of one the free gift came upon all men unto δικαιωσιν ζωης, justification of life. Now this very blessing he tells us Abraham received, not by works, but by faith.

And in the eleventh verse of the fourth chapter we are told " he received the sign of circumcision, a seal of the righteousness of the faith which he had yet being uncircumcised." The word which in this verse is translated righteousness is the same in the original as that translated justification in verse 25 of the same chapter, and in verse 18 of the following chapter, as any one may see by looking into his Greek Testament; and Dr. Adam Clarke says it " is best rendered *justification*, as expressing that *pardon* and *salvation* offered to us in the Gospel." A righteous *act*, a righteous *state*, and the *act* and *state* of pardon; all are expressed by words, all of which are derived from the same root and that root is Δικαιος, which means *just*, or *right*. Hence we have dikaiothentes, being justified; dikaiosune, the state of being upright; dikaiosune justice, righteousness; and dikaiosin, justification. This word has always reference to law, and is used to express something in harmony with, or contrary to, law; as righteousness and unrighteousness. Now, why such a word should be used to express the *act* and *state* of pardon, why the words justified, and pardoned, should be used interchangeably and synonymously; why they should be used to express one and the same thing, as they certainly are by this Apostle in the Scriptures now under consideration, seems at first sight unaccountable: for pardon has nothing to do with law, unless to set it at defiance; at least this is true of pardon as usually understood. For instance, if one should take away my property by fraud, and I should pardon him fully and sincerely, the law would take no notice of my pardon, but would hold him guilty, and pronounce sentence just as readily after I had pardoned as before; and this is alike true both of human and divine law. Why, then, is the guilty culprit said to be justified when God pardons him? The fact is, God's pardon is like no other pardon, because it is in harmony with law; and it is in harmony with law, because, though the guilty is pardoned, the claims of the law are satisfied, are fully met, by the atonement. Though the sinner is pardoned there is no compromise with justice, its claims are fully met, it is satisfied; and the sinner now stands acquitted in the eye of the law. Hence the same Apostle says, "There is, therefore, now, no condemnation to them that are in Christ Jesus." And again, "Who shall lay anything to the charge of God's elect? It is God that justifieth; who is he that condemneth? It is Christ that died, yea, rather, that is risen again, who is even at the right hand of God, who also maketh intercession for us." None but God Almighty can pardon thus, no other being can possibly do so; and there was only one way in which he could do it, namely, by an atonement; "For," says the same Apostle, "If there had been a law given which could have given life, verily righteousness should have been by the law." Gal. iii. 21. But there was no such law, it was only by an atonement, according to the same authority, that God could be "just" and at the same time *justify* or *pardon*. Rom. iii 26. And while this could be done only by an atonement, that atonement could only be made in the way it was made; "there remaineth no more sacrifice for sin," says the same authority.

Now, then, let us sum up, and we shall find the amount to be this. The infant has the same qualification for baptism that Abraham had for circumcision, and that qualification is justification; and it receives baptism for the same *reason* that Abraham received circumcision, namely, because it is *justified;* and it receives baptism for the same *purpose* that Abraham received circumcision, namely, as the "sign" and "seal" of "righteousness," or "justification," previously received: and this right to, and qualification for, baptism, it has from the same source, the very same source, from which Abraham received his right to, and qualification for circumcision. The only difference in the case is this: Abraham received justification conditionally, viz., by faith, but the infant receives justification unconditionally; Abraham's justification removed the condemnation brought upon him by his own transgressions, as well as the condemnation brought upon him by the original offence; while the infant's justification simply removes the condemnation brought upon it by the original apostacy, it having no act of its own; but the result of justification in each case is precisely the same, viz., this, the justified party in each case, is placed right with regard to the law; for, as we before observed, justification, or pardon, is a relative change, by which the relation of the justified party is changed with regard to the law, and consequently, with regard to the Lawgiver. In a word, all who are justified stand accepted before God the judge, and in the eye of the law, so that there is no condemnation for the past. Hence infants being thus justified through the atonement, or as Paul expresses it in the text quoted above "through the righteousness of one," even Christ, they have the same right to the seal of the covenant, that believing adults have, the same right that Abraham had when he was justified, and received the seal accordingly. Now as this qualification is received unconditionally, it follows, as we said before, that if one infant has it all have it; and as this qualification is from Christ, and unconditional, it follows, too, that the parents have nothing to do either with qualifying or disqualifying them; as they have justification through Christ, and are thus qualified for baptism despite the sin of their first parents, so they have this qualification and right, despite the disobedience of their second parents; they are not qualified for baptism either by the faith or the holiness of their parents but by the atonement of Christ; if the parents have faith enough to present their children for baptism, that answers all purposes, so far as the children are concerned; and being thus presented, it is the duty of the minister of Christ to baptize them, and to enjoin it upon the parents to teach them to fear and worship that God to whom they have now consecrated them in holy baptism; and to remind them that they are bound by the most sacred obligations, and now by consistency itself, to consecrate themselves to that God to whom they have consecrated their children. I have utterly failed to discover where any minister finds his authority for refusing baptism to any infant that may be presented to him by its parents for that purpose.

Finally, from the Scriptures here quoted, I think we are inevitably forced to the following conclusions. All infants have, through the atonement, unconditionally a *right* to, and a *qualification* for, baptism; and that qualification is the very same qualification that Abraham had for circumcision, the very same that believing adults have for baptism, namely, justification; and this justification, of course, does the very same thing for the infant that it does for the believing adult, namely, this, it puts it right with regard to the law, by removing the condemnatory sentence of the law, for this is the sole office of justification, whether the party be an infant or an adult. Thus infants, through the atonement, sustain precisely the same relation to the law, and to God the judge of all, that believing adults do; the very same that Abraham did when he was justified; and that is a justified relation. Hence we see why it is that infants, as well as Abraham, "received the sign of circumcision," which Paul says was "a seal of the *righteousness*," or *justification* previously had. Now when we know, upon Scripture authority, that God commanded *Abraham* and *infant children* to be circumcised, and know, too, on the same authority, that circumcision was a seal of justification previously had, we thereby know that infants as well as Abraham were justified, or they would not have received the seal of justification, for that would be affixing the seal of justification to those who were not justified; which would not only be an unmeaning act, but a delusive act. Nay, it would be affixing the seal to an untruth!

The conclusion here reached secures the salvation of all infants, dying as such. Those who reject this conclusion are shut up to one of two conclusions, viz., that all infants are lost, or a certain part of them; and if they adopt the latter conclusion, they thereby represent God as damning infants whom he might have saved, for if he saved a part he certainly might have saved all, seeing all were alike incapable of offering resistance to the means employed for their salvation; and if they do not like this or the preceding conclusion, then they must adopt infant baptism; for if the infant is justified and fitted for heaven without its own act, it certainly may be, and is fitted for baptism without its own act. Thus we see that there is a close connection between infant baptism and infant salvation on the one hand; and na equally close connection between Antipedobaptism, and infant damnation on the other!

Again, Antipedobaptists "will baptize on profession," and on profession only. That is, they will baptize one who "indulges a hope that he has met with a change." But what does this mean? Why, it means just this, if it means anything to the purpose; he indulges a hope that he is justified, or pardoned. So that they have not even his word for it, but merely his hope; and upon this evidence they baptize him. But we have God's word for it that the infant is "justified freely by his grace through the redemption that is in Christ Jesus." And on this evidence we baptize it! This, then, is the difference; by so much as God's testimony is better than that man's professed hope, by so much is our authority for baptizing the infant better than their authority for baptizing the adult! And in the same way we reach the conclusion, that no adult under heaven has as clear a claim to the rite of baptism as has the infant; because we have God's testimony in favor of the justification of the infant, while we have only man's testimony in favor of the justification of the adult, and that the testimony of the interested party, the party seeking baptism; and the party judging in the case is also interested, being under the influence of a desire to make accessions to his church and party! Nor does the preponderance in our favor stop here, for we not only have God's testimony in favor of the infant's qualification for baptism, but we have his command to apply to the infant the very same seal that he commanded to be applied to the adult, viz., the seal of the covenant, the seal of justification obtained through the atonement; which justification is obtained by the adult conditionally, and by the infant unconditionally. It follows that he who will have better authority for anything that he does, than we have for baptizing the infant, must have better than the testimony and command of the Almighty! Truly they are seriously defective in Bible knowledge who exclude infants from Christian baptism: and I do not hesitate to say, that Antipedobaptism originated in an ignorance of, and is at variance with, some of the first and most glorious principles of the Christian system; and upon that ignorance it is that it depends principally for its propagation; and it is high time that this error and the ignorance of which it is the offspring should be driven out of Christendom! Infants are redeemed. Jesus claims them all as the purchase of his blood, and says "Suffer little children to come unto me, and forbid them not, for of such is the kingdom of God." And every minister of Jesus should unite with Jesus in rebuking those who forbid their being brought to Jesus, and should iterate and reiterate the words of Jesus, saying, "Forbid them not." And they should unite with Paul in uttering that glorious truth upon which we have been commenting, and upon which we delight to dwell; "Therefore, as by the offence of one, judgment came upon all men to condemnation, even so by the righteousness of one the free gift came upon all men unto justification of life." These truths should be uttered by Zion's watchmen joyously and incessantly; and should come pealing like thunder from every part of Zion's walls. And they should be taken up by the inhabitants of Zion and uttered with such rapturous joy that their voices commingling should be as the sound of many waters: then should the dolorous, owl-like voice of the Antipedobaptist be heard no more!

If by the sin of our first parents their posterity were excluded from the Kingdom of God without their own act, and are not restored by the righteousness of Christ without their own act, it will follow that Adam did more to destroy than Christ did to save, and if so, Paul uttered an untruth when he said, " Where sin abounded grace did much more abound." But as we cannot adopt either of these conclusions, we are forced, in this way also, to adopt the conclusion which we claim to have established, viz., that the condemnation which came by Adam's sin, is removed by the justification which came by Christ's righteousness; and the parties who by that condemnation were excluded from God's Kingdom, and, consequently, from eternal life, by a non-existence, are by this justification restored thereto. And if they are justified and restored to God's Kingdom through the atonement, we may well say in the language of Peter, " Can any forbid water that these should not be baptized;" for a justification received without faith qualifies for circumcision or for baptism just as much as a justification received by faith; for justification is the same whether received conditionally or unconditionally.

In the light of these teachings we are prepared, I trust, to see more clearly, and to appreciate more fully, the following blessed and altogether glorious words of our Almighty Saviour! "And they brought young children to him that he should touch them: and his disciples rebuked those that brought them. But when Jesus saw it he was much displeased, and said unto them,

" Suffer the little children to come unto me, and forbid them not, for of such is the kingdom of God. Verily I say unto you, whosoever shall not receive the Kingdom of God as a little child, he shall not enter therein. And he took them in his arms, put his hands upon them, and blessed them."—Mark x. 13–17.

Now, with this passage before us, we will call attention to, and make a few remarks upon, the following particulars, which may be considered the more prominent features of the passage. It will be remembered that Anabaptists speak of "unconscious babes" as though neither God nor man could do anything for them; but the following particulars convey a very different idea.

The first particular to which we call attention is this; *infants are susceptible of the divine blessing*, for we are told that " Jesus took them in his arms, put his hands upon them, and blessed them." I say *infants*, for Luke calls these "little children" *infants.*

Now let us not look upon all this as mere form; when " the Lord of life and glory" pronounces blessing upon the infant that is brought to him by the parent's hands, and by the parent's heart, his utterances are not mere unmeaning words; his blessing means something! Let it be remembered, too, that it is by his righteousness that " the free gift came upon all men unto justification of life," and that " the blessing of the Lord, it maketh rich," and infants have that blessing. Yes, they have it, for we have heard " the Lord of life and glory" pronounce his blessing upon them, even upon the infants that were brought unto him. Who, then, would refuse to bring their infant children to this " Lord of life and glory ?" and when parents bring their infant children unto him, Who will dare to "forbid them?" We know none in Christendom who would do so but Antipedobaptists! Let it be remembered, too, that if one infant is capable or susceptible of receiving the "blessing of the LORD," all are; for all infants are alike incapable of offering resistance to the divine will. O let not parents or ministers resist that will, by doing what those did with whom Jesus was "much displeased;" and remember, he is as much displeased with that act now as he was then! But rather than admit that Jesus is capable of blessing the soul of an infant, Antipedobaptists have invented the marvellous idea that the infants here spoken of were brought to Jesus to have some bodily disease healed! By this invention they represent the disciples as forbidding their being brought for this purpose, a thing they never did, for it was customary to bring all manner of sick persons to Jesus: and they represent Jesus as insisting that diseased infants should be brought to him for the purpose of being healed, and as giving this reason, "for of such is the Kingdom of God." Certainly this objection does not deserve further notice.

We next call attention to the phrase, "Of such is the Kingdom of God." Now if we understand this phrase, "Kingdom of God," or as St. Matthew expresses it, "Kingdom of heaven," to mean the future home of God's people, then these words of Jesus assure us that infants are heirs of that Kingdom with all those adults whose names are written in heaven. But if we are to understand by this phrase, the Church of God upon the earth, then we are taught to recognize infants as properly constituted members of that Church, which they certainly were under both the patriarchal and Mosaic dispensations; and surely the perfected Gospel dispensation will not exclude from their place in the church those infants whom the less perfect dispensations received into that place! And if we understand Jesus to teach us, as we certainly must, that infants are, through the atonement, members of the heavenly kingdom, then certainly we cannot exclude them from the earthly kingdom. Hence, whatever way we understand the phrase we must understand our blessed Lord as placing infants in his Kingdom, which "is not of this world." And if we understand him as teaching that adults who constitute his Kingdom must resemble little children, as some Antipedobaptists would interpret the words "of such," certainly their cause will gain nothing by it, for by this interpretation they make infants *model Christians!* And if they are *model Christians*, we desire to know upon what ground they refuse to baptize them!

"A more correct translation," says Mr. Watson, on the place, "would be, *For to such belongeth the Kingdom of God.*"

We may now glance at the words, "Verily I say unto you, whosoever shall not receive the Kingdom of God as a little child, he shall not enter therein." Now if we take the ground that infants do not receive, do not share in the Kingdom of God, how could our blessed Lord teach, as he here does, that we must all receive it as they do? And unless we attribute this absurdity to our Lord, we must understand him as teaching that infants do receive the kingdom, do belong to the kingdom of God. But how do infants receive the Kingdom of God? Like a pharisee, by fasting twice in the week and paying tithe of all that they possess? Certainly not.

How then do they receive it? By works of righteousness which they have done? By no means; the helpless infant has neither tithe nor works of any kind. How then do they receive it? By merit of any kind? No, not by merit of any kind. How then do they receive it? Paul tells us, in the words which we have quoted several times already; they receive it as a "free gift;" they were "justified freely by his grace;" "the free gift came upon all unto justification of life." And just so every child of man must receive it, or not at all. Only in the case of adults who are accountable for actions of their own, and must now be treated as moral agents, faith is required as a condition. But still they receive the Kingdom of God as a "free gift." Still it is by grace they are saved through faith, and that not of themselves; "it is the gift of God." Here we are again taught that infants and believing adults receive the same kingdom, and both receive it as a "free gift," and for precisely the same reason each is entitled to the seal of the covenant, the seal of justification already received as a "free gift," through the atonement. How then dare any one rebuke those who bring their beloved infants to Jesus in holy baptism, seeing they are his by redemption, his by justification, as truly as are believing adults? For those who did so before Jesus uttered the above words, there might be some excuse; but for those who do so in defiance of these teachings and reproofs of Jesus it is difficult, very difficult, if at all possible, to find any excuse. Let them remember, however, that with such conduct "Jesus was much displeased," and let all who are rebuked by them for bringing their children to Jesus, treat their rebukes as Jesus did.

In speaking of the qualification of *infants* for baptism, it will be seen that we did not find that qualification in the goodness of their moral nature. Our teachings here are not Pelagian, nor are they in the least tainted with Pelagianism. It is quite certain that infants come into the world with a nature morally depraved. The word of God is neither equivocal nor obscure on that point. Man is made to declare that fact with his own lips, in these words: " I was shapen in iniquity; and in sin did my mother conceive me." " The wicked are estranged from the womb." God has not told us *when* or *how* he *rectifies* the moral nature of the infant. Hence it were folly for man to undertake to tell what God has not told. But he has told us that the condemnation brought upon it by the apostacy of the first parents is removed by an unconditional *justification* vouchsafed through the atonement. And this relative change which sets it right with regard to the law, is its qualification for baptism. Although it is not for us to say, nor does our argument require us to say, why God has not spoken as clearly with regard to the positive, as he has with regard to the relative change, we may observe, that the relative change could take place before the child had a positive existence, but the positive change could not. And it is proper to observe, too, that when adults are justified their moral nature is very far from being perfectly pure; they are not then cleansed from all the natural uncleanness, they are not sanctified wholly. Why this is so, God has not told us; the fact, however, we must submit to in each case. It is enough for us to know that if God calls away that infant, or that newly justified adult, he will make each mete for an inheritance among the saints in light, for "without holiness no one shall see the Lord." But why, or to what extent the further work is left conditional, we cannot tell. We have gone as far as facts and revelation guide us.

CHAPTER XV.

The Argument from Apostolic Practice—The Apostles Baptized the Believing Father and his House—Remarks on the Greek words *Oikos* and *Oikia*—Taylor is quoted—Some further remarks with regard to the Origin and History of the Anabaptists.

We will now glance at the Apostolic practice as recorded in the New Testament; from which we learn that the Apostles not only baptized the head of the house, when converted, but the family also. Hence, when the Jailor believed, we are told that "He was baptized, he and all his straightway." In like manner, we are told when Lydia believed, "She was baptized, and her household." And St. Paul says: "I baptized also the house of Stephanus."

But in all these and many other families similarly spoken of in the New Testament, the Antipedobaptists can find no children; they will have it that all these families were as childless as are their own churches! Just as soon as the sacred writers tell us of a man that was baptized, "he and all his," they are ready to say, "write this man childless!" But, as Mr. Watson says, "The great difficulty with Baptists is to make a house for Lydia without any children at all, young or old." And I do not know but they think they have succeeded admirably, when they tell us about certain journeymen dyers, whom they conjecture were "employed in preparing the purple she sold!" Of these journeymen, however, no mortal ever heard anything, but what the Baptists tell us; and, what is still worse, the Baptists themselves never heard of such men; it is all *made up!* And it only tends, as Mr. Watson further observes, "to mark more strikingly the helplessness of the attempt to torture this passage in favor of an opinion."

As the objections of the Antipedobaptists to what has been said with regard to family baptisms by other writers, have been frequently and fully answered; and as it is, and has been, our purpose not to follow the beaten track, we will simply say, just here, that it was Lydia and her *oikos* that was baptized, not Lydia and her journeymen dyers. And when she was baptized, and her *oikos*, she besought the Apostles, saying, "If ye have judged me to be faithful to the Lord, come into my *oikon*." It was not her *oikia*, but her *oikos*, that was baptized! Our opponents will please look into their Greek Testaments and see if this is not so. We beg to remind them, too, that no man speaking the Greek language, especially if he were a scholar, as Luke was, would tell us of the baptism of Lydia and her *oikos*, when he meant Lydia and her journeymen dyers! Moreover, while the sacred historian gives us a minute account of Lydia's conversion, he does not say a word about the conversion of her journeymen dyers! In short, all this talk about Lydia's journeymen dyers is as ridiculous as it is gratuitous. Nor does the sacred historian say a word about the conversion of Lydia's *oikos;* he simply tells us that, being converted, "she was baptized and her *oikos;*" for, there being no Antipedobaptists in those days, it was entirely unnecessary to say more; seeing it was the well known and divinely established usage to extend the initiatory rite to the children of the initiated parent. But no such privilege belonged to the employees of the believer, simply because their employer was a believer; and if Lydia's hired men had been converted, Luke would have told us of their conversion when he told us of their baptism, just as he told us of the conversion of Lydia when he told us of her baptism. But Luke has simply told us of the conversion of Lydia and of her baptism, and of the baptism of her *oikos* in consequence. And every Christian in those days, when told of Lydia's conversion and baptism, knew why her *oikos* were baptized, just as a Jew knew why the *oikos* of a Jew were circumcised. Every Jew knew that Ishmael was circumcised when his father Abraham was; though the former was then "thirteen years old." And it was equally well known that Isaac was circumcised when "eight days old." And this practice continued among all the worshippers of the true God from that time till baptism took the place of circumcision. Here, then, we have this fact, viz: that circumcision was, by divine command, extended to the children of believing parents from the age of eight days to that of thirteen years, *without any reference to their own act!* Now, when Lydia received the seal of the covenant, her children, her *oikos*, also received it, just as did the *oikos* of Abraham after their father received it. Here is the record, Gen. xvii. 26: "In the self-same day was Abraham circumcised, and Ishmael, his son;" and if Abraham had had other children, of course they, too, would have received the seal of the covenant the self-same day that Abraham and Ishmael did. Now, in precisely the same way it was, and for the same reason, that the *oikos* of Lydia received the seal the self-same day that their mother did. Agreeably to this exactly, are the teachings of Paul when he says the children are holy, that is sanctified, or consecrated to God in baptism even where one of the parents is a believer; so that we have both his teaching and practice for baptizing children, even where only one of the parents is a believer, and brings her children with her. These are facts that bid defiance to all that can be said by the advocates of mere novelty!

Although what is here said is, we believe, a sufficient explanation and defence of all the family baptisms referred to, we will, nevertheless, glance at the baptism of the Jailor's family, as it is recorded in Acts xvi., because we think a more critical examination of the record will elicit information not obtained without a reference to the original.

If you will look into your Greek Testament, you will find that the reading is as follows: Verse 30: "Sirs, what must I do to be saved? And they said, Believe on the Lord Jesus Christ and thou shalt be saved, and thy *oikos.* And they spake unto him the word of the Lord, and to all that were in his *oikia.* And he took them the same hour of the night and washed their stripes; and was baptized, *he and all his,*" not all the *oikia*, but "*all his.*" "And when he had brought them into his *oikon*, he set meat before them, and rejoiced, believing in God with all his *oikon.*"

Now, having before us this brief and clear exhibit of the sacred narrative, in which every one can see the words as they are varied in the original, but not in the common text, we call attention to the following particulars: First, the promise and its condition read thus: "Believe on the Lord Jesus Christ and thou shalt be saved, and thy *oikos*." Second, "they spake unto him the word of the Lord, and to all that were in his *oikia*," not *oikos*, you will observe. Third, he did believe, "and was baptized, *he and all his*." In Mark, it is not said that he and all his *oikia* were baptized, but "*he and all his*." The promise was to him and his *oikos*, children; the word was preached to him and to all that were in his *oikia*, not only to him, but to all his household, all who were present. But we are not told that any believed except the Jailor, nor are we told that any were baptized save "*he and all his*." His children were baptized with him, precisely as Paul had promised; but the others present, and not believing, though the word was preached to them, had no such privilege; they were not baptized, as were "he and all his." Now, he brought them into his *oikon* and "set meat before them, and rejoiced, believing in God with all his *oikon*." Having obtained salvation, and he and his family being baptized, he prepared this eucharistic feast, and "rejoiced with all his house, believing in God." *Egalliasato panoiki pepisteukos to Theo.* Believing in God as he did, or having believed, he rejoiced with his house, or, as some express it, at the head of his house. *Panoiki* is differently rendered, but the whole of the 34th verse, taken together, is plain enough; the whole house partook of his joy and he of theirs; but the believing is peculiarly predicated of him.

But I desire more especially to call attention to the words *oikos* and *oikia*. The promise was to the former, the preaching to the latter, and the baptism was ad ministered to *him* and *all his.* These are the facts as recorded.

Mr. Taylor, in his admirable work on Baptism, entitled "Facts and Evidences," says, p. 90: "When the Philippian Jailor enquired, 'What must I do to be saved?' the Apostle answered, 'Believe on the Lord Jesus Christ and thou shalt be saved and thy house.' The *oikia*, servants of the Jailor, heard the Word; but we do not read that one of the oikia was baptized, saved, but this we do read of the Jailor, and of *all his house;* which is exactly what the Apostle foretold." It will be seen that Mr. Taylor marks the same distinction between the words *oikos* and *oikia* that we have pointed out above. Again, on p. 60, speaking of the baptism of Stephanus, he says: "Scripture says his family was baptized; I, therefore, believe that fact—Scripture says nothing of the baptism of his household, I, therefore, do not believe it. *But I will believe it whenever a passage of Scripture shall be produced in which* HOUSEHOLD, *oikia*, is connected with baptism." Here this ripe scholar, after the most careful investigation, tells us that he has failed to find a single instance on record where a man and his *oikia*, household, are said to have been baptized; but he does find it recorded that Lydia and her *oikos* were baptized, and that the Jailor and his *oikos* were baptized; but although we are told that the Apostle preached the Word to the Jailor's *oikia* we are not told that his *oikia* were baptized. The promise was to him and his children, *oikos*, and when he believed *he* and *his* were baptized according to promise!

Following the above remarks, Mr. Taylor proceeds thus: "The mischance that our translators should have used the terms *house* and *household* interchangeably, though Scripture preserves the distinction, is glaring respecting the family of Onesiphorus, 2 Timothy i. 16, and iv. 19. The Greek word in one text is rendered 'house,' and in the other 'household,' notwithstanding the same persons are intended. Our translators also have used one word, *household,* to express both the *family* and *household* of Stephanus, though Scripture uses two words in order to make the distinction, and certainly *does not mean* the same persons. This has produced confusion, and various weak and inconsistent arguments." To this fact we have called attention in the narrative of the Jailor's conversion and baptism, where we have shown that the sacred historian has used the words *oikos* and *oikia,* both of which are rendered *house,* though the historian predicates of the one what he does not of the other.

So convinced is Mr. Taylor of the truthfulness and the importance of this distinction, and of the fixedness of the meaning of the word *oikos,* both in the Old and New Testaments, that he wholly rests his argument in favor of Infant Baptism upon this single point. Hence, on page 14, he says: "The argument is brought to this point: the Old Testament writers use the term *House* in the sense of *family,* with a special reference to INFANTS; the New Testament writers use the term *House* exactly in the same sense as the Old Testament writers; therefore, when the New Testament writers say that they *baptized houses,* they mean to say that they baptized INFANTS." After the most laborious investigation, and after quoting numerous texts of scripture, both from the Old and New Testaments, and after producing a great variety of arguments, such as none but a scholar and a thinker could produce, and all to establish the above proposition, he reaches such conclusions as the following, which I find upon page 89: "Being myself convinced that the Apostles practised infant baptism, and that the evangelist meant to tell us so, I affirm that the *natural* import of the term *oikos*, family, includes *children of all ages.* In proof, I offer *fifty* examples; if *fifty* are not sufficient, I offer *a hundred;* if *a hundred* are not sufficient, two hundred; if *two hundred* are not sufficient, four hundred. I affirm that *oikos* VERY OFTEN *expresses* the presence of infants; of this I offer *fifty* examples, and if we admit classical instances, *fifty* more. Euripides alone affords half the number, though he frequently uses *domos* instead of *oikos.* More than *three hundred* instances *have been examined* which have proved perfectly satisfactory." He now goes on to show that when the sacred writers tell us of the baptism of a man and his *oikos*, they thereby convey to us the idea of infant baptism *more undeniably* than they could, perhaps, in any other way. In proof of this he quotes the following facts, thus: "What terms could the evangelists have used to satisfy us of the apostolic practice of infant baptism? Had they said, 'We baptize *infants;*' Origen says this, and Baptists immediately exclaim, '*Metaphorical* infants! *metaphorical* infants!' Had they said, 'We baptize children,' as the apostles Paul and John, and Clement of Alexandria say, they answer, '*Metaphorical* children!'" Hence he concludes that when the sacred writers use the word *oikos* as they have done, they thereby put the fact of infant baptism more effectually beyond the possibility of evasion than they would have done if they had only used the word *infants;* for the word family, or *oikos*, must include infants and little ones; and we may more plausibly talk about *metaphorical* infants, or children, than we could about *metaphorical families!* So true it is that the Bible is right not only as to the ideas, which it conveys to us, but also as to the words which it employs for that purpose. The truth is, no words could be used that would prevent certain people from rejecting the right and embracing the wrong. Some people will be wrong anyhow!

After quoting many texts in the Old Testament, the same author quotes the following: Ruth iv. 11, 13: "The LORD make the woman that is come into thine house like Rachel and like Lea, which two did build the house of Israel: and do thou worthily in Ephratah: and be famous in Bethlehem: and let thine house be like the house of Pharez, whom Tamar bare unto Judah, of the seed which the Lord shall give thee of this young woman." "It is not possible," continues our author, "by any form of words whatever, to express INFANTS more decidedly than by these applications of the term HOUSE: and if there were no other text in the Old Testament, this last alone is sufficient to establish the proposition that the term *house* in the Old Testament language MUST mean an *infant.* The *building up of the house* of Israel is *infant* child-bearing. Thy HOUSE—the 'SEED which the Lord SHALL GIVE THEE of this young woman' MUST mean an *infant.* This is the national and acknowledged language used by 'all the people that were in the gate,' not by the vulgar only, but by those well instructed; by the *elders.*" Thus it is that this writer establishes the fact, viz: that this word *oikos*, house, conveys the idea of *infants*, or children, both in the Old and New Testaments. The Spirit that inspired and guided the writers of the Old Testament to use this word for the purpose of conveying this idea, also inspired and guided the New Testament writers to use it for the same purpose. Now, seeing this word had this fixed and universally understood meaning among that people for some two thousand years, was it possible for them to misunderstand one of their own writers when he told them that he baptized the Jailor and his *oikos*, Lydia and her *oikos*, Stephanus and his *oikos?* I say, was it possible for them to understand him otherwise than that he baptized the man and his children, or the woman and her children, as the case might be? And, waiving the consideration of inspiration, we ask, was it possible for a Jewish writer to tell this people that he baptized a man and his house, if he did not mean a man and his children, especially infants? And the supposition becomes the more impossible, when it is remembered not only that his *oikos* meant his children, but that it was the divinely appointed usage of that people, and had been so for some two thousand years, to apply the seal to the children when it was applied to the parent. The fact is, it seems impossible for any one that is not shamefully ignorant of the Bible and history, to doubt the meaning of the historic records of the New Testament with regard to the baptism of certain individuals and their families.

After filling nearly one hundred pages with "facts and evidences" in favor of infant baptism, this writer closes his admirable work with the following remarks, which we think may be useful just here:

"I close these researches upon the SUBJECT OF CHRISTIAN BAPTISM with two inferences.

"1. The Christian Church in the North, in the South, in the East, and in the West, NEVER DID REFUSE BAPTISM TO INFANTS. Are the Baptists, then, wiser than all the world? than all the *faithful men* of apostolic ages, and than all their contemporaries? Is it likely that they alone, of all the millions of Christians of every period and nation, in spite of these 'FACTS and EVIDENCES,' should be the *only* persons who have elicited Scriptural truth?

"2. In all Christian Churches, baptism is a *consecration to the Trinity!* Not one uses any form of words—the Baptists themselves do not use any form of words, in the administration of baptism, allusive to the *burial* of the person baptized, as they say Christ was *buried.* Had our Lord intended such allusion, He would have said so. . . . . I adhere to the initiatory words of Christ as the best and greatest authority on the subject; for it is very extraordinary that in a religion having but *two* rites, they should *both* point at the same thing. The death of the Saviour is clearly the primary and direct purport of the Lord's Supper. Is it likely or credible that the *primary* and *direct* purport of baptism should also be the death of the Saviour? But if in the initiatory rite there be a commemoration of the *interposing Deity,* and in the Lord's Supper a commemoration of the *interposing humanity*—if for this reason consecration to the Deity is sufficient by one act, and ought not to be repeated, while devotedness to Jesus, as Lord of all, is frequently renewed, and to be repeated continually, then there is between the two rites that distinction which was evidently intended, and which it well becomes all professors of our common faith to retain to the latest generation."

It is a remarkable, and a very telling fact, that those scholars who have been most thorough in their investigations on the subject of baptism have, as the result of their investigations, been most confident in their conclusions. Hence the editor of Calmet's Dictionary, like Baxter and many others, has utterly failed to find anything clearly in favor of Anabaptist notions, while his vast accumulation of FACTS and EVIDENCES are directly and irreconcilably opposed to them. As an antiquarian he searches ancient churches, catacombs, and other places, and there finds monuments of the artistic skill, and of the piety, sentiments, and practice of the ancient Christians; monuments which have stood there from primitive times, bearing their unchangeable and unmistakable testimony both as to the *mode* and *subjects* of baptism during the early and following ages of the Christian Church, and in every instance they testify that Anabaptist notions are *novelties!* These ancient works of art represent baptism as being administered by *pouring;* and the ancient inscriptions testify to the baptism of children, after this manner: "To Aristus who lived eight months: NEWLY BAPTIZED, he went off the first of the nones of June, A. D. 389: Timasius and Promotorus being Consuls." The original is in Latin, and this is the translation which our author gives us. This is only one out of the many similar inscriptions which he furnishes. As a philologist he searches with equal diligence, and discovers that the words which refer to the subject in hand were fixed and unmistakable in their meaning, and that they bear an equally decisive and unequivocal testimony against the same novelties; and that their testimony in favor of the views here contended for is not less decisive and unequivocal. And, finally, as a student of history, he discovers that "the Christian Churches in the North, in the South, in the East, and in the West, NEVER DID REFUSE BAPTISM TO INFANTS!" And finding that neither he nor any other man, ancient or modern, could discover what Antipedobaptists claim to have discovered, he asks: "Is it likely that they alone, of all the millions of Christians of every period and nation, in spite of these FACTS and EVIDENCES, should be the *only* persons who have elicited Scripture truth!" But startling as is this question, it will become still more startling if put in this form, which is really the proper form: "Is it likely that the fanatics of Germany, such as Thomas Munzer, Conrad Grebel, John Matthias, and John Boccold, should discover what all the learned, the wise, and the good, both ancient and modern, have failed to discover?" This is really the question; for to the parties here mentioned we trace the Antipedobaptist notions, and beyond these parties we find them not. If the advocates of these notions can find them prior to these fanatics, let them tell us when, and where!

But lest any should impose upon their neighbors by bold assertion instead of argument, which is not at all an unfrequent occurrence, we will here furnish a few of the facts of history.

To escape the storm which was now driving down with terrible fury from the "seven mountains upon which the woman sitteth," Luther was carried to the ancient Castle of Wartburg, where he remained for some twelve months. During his stay there the Reformation progressed, but there arose a new set of reformers claiming to be prophets, and like certain reformers in olden times boasting great things. The good Elector of Saxony being both alarmed and puzzled, wrote Luther. The great Reformer soon comprehended the matter, and replied thus: "Your Electoral grace has been accustomed for many years to seek for relics in every country. God has granted your desires, and has sent you, without expense or trouble, a complete *cross*, with nails, lances, and scourges . . . . grace and prosperity to the new relic! . . . . Let your Highness only without fear extend your arms, and allow the nails to pierce the flesh! . . . . . I have always expected that Satan would send us this plague." This plague first appeared in the little town of Zwickau. The following account of it is from D'Aubigne's History of the Reformation, 1846. W. R. McPhun, Glasgow. Page 579:

"There dwelt in this town some men who, excited by the manifestation of the great events which then agitated the public mind in Christendom, aspired to the possession of direct revelations from the Divine Being, instead of seeking with simplicity the sanctification of the heart, and who pretended that they were called to complete the Reformation of which Luther had weakly sketched the design. 'For what good purpose is it,' said they, 'to attach one's self so exclusively to the Bible? The Bible! Always the Bible! Can the Bible speak to us? Is it not insufficient for our instruction? If God had wished to instruct us by means of a book, would he not have sent us a Bible from heaven? It is by the Spirit alone that we can be enlightened. God Himself thus speaks to us. God Himself reveals to us what we ought to do and what we ought to say.' A simple cloth manufacturer named Nicolas Stork, declared that the Angel Gabriel had appeared to him during the night, and that, after having communicated many things which he could not yet reveal, the Angel had said: 'Thou thyself shalt sit upon my throne.' One of the former students at Wittemberg, called Mark Stubner, united himself to Stork, and immediately abandoned his studies; because, as he said, he received directly from God the gift of interpreting the Holy Scriptures. Mark Thomas, another cloth manufacturer, also joined the party; while a new adept, Thomas Munzer, a man of a fantastic disposition, imparted a regular organization to the body of this new sect. Stork, wishing to follow the example of Christ, chose from among his adherents twelve apostles and seventy-two disciples." After telling us somewhat of their prophesyings and of their doings, our historian thus proceeds: "Nicolas Haussman, to whom Luther bore this elegant testimony—'That which we teach he does'—was then the pastor of Zwickau. This worthy man did not allow himself to be carried away by the assumptions of these false prophets. He opposed the innovations which Stork and his adherents were anxious to introduce, and the two deacons of the church acted in unison with their pastor. . . . . They formed regular organizations, wherein destructive doctrines were acknowledged, and the minds of the people became highly excited." The civil authorities interfering, these fanatics met with an opposition which checked their progress, and Nicolas Stork, Mark Thomas, and Mark Stubner, started for Wittemberg.

"They arrived in this celebrated town," continues our historian, "on the 27th of December, 1521. Stork marched first, imitating the step and bearing of a common soldier, while Thomas and Stubner followed behind him. The troubles which reigned in Wittemberg favored the designs of these strangers. The youths of the academy, and the citizens, at the time in a state of much agitation, composed, as it were, a soil prepared for the operations of the new prophets. Hence, believing themselves sure of their support, they immediately waited upon the professors of the university, in order to obtain their concurrence. 'We are,' said the strangers, 'sent from God to give instruction to the people. We hold familiar conversation with the Lord, and we are acquainted with the events that are to come to pass: in a word, we are apostles and prophets, and we appeal, in this matter, to Doctor Luther. This singular language amazed the doctors of the university. 'Who has ordained you to preach?' enquired Melancthon of Stubner, his former pupil, whom he received into his house: 'Our Lord God.' 'Have you written any books?' 'Our Lord God has forbidden me to do so.' Melancthon was thunderstruck; equally amazed and alarmed. . . . . Stork, whose character was restless, very soon quitted the town of Wittemberg, but Stubner remained there. Animated with an ardent desire of proselytism, he visited every district of the town, speaking sometimes to one person, sometimes to another (their children but too closely adhere to the practice of their ancestors), and several of his hearers acknowledged him as a prophet sent from God. He addressed himself particularly to a Swabian named Cellarius, a friend of Melancthon, who kept a school wherein he gave instructions in letters to a great number of young people, and who very soon fully recognized the mission of the new prophets.

"Melancthon became more and more uncertain and disquieted in his mind. It was not so much the visions of the prophets from Zwickau which disturbed his imagination, as the new doctrine they professed upon the sacrament of baptism." Mark, it was A NEW DOCTRINE! What it was we shall see pretty soon.

"Circumstances became more and more serious at Wittemberg. Carlstadt rejected several of the doctrines professed by the new prophets, and in particular their *Anabaptism.*" But things grew worse and worse, and the friends of the Reformation were now more afraid of these fanatical Anabaptists than they were of Rome itself; for the enemies of the truth were shrewd enough to charge their fanatical doings and their wild insubordination to Luther and his followers, in a word, to the Reformation.

Meantime many communications reached Luther in the Castle of Wartburg, and he was evidently well convinced both as to the *nature* and *danger* of the work that was going on. "I throw myself," he exclaimed, "in the dust while creeping towards the grace of the Eternal, and I beseech him to allow his name to be still connected with this work, and that if something impure has mingled in its operations, he will remember that I am a weak and sinful man." Finally, "upon the third of March, he rose with the resolution to quit the Castle of Wartburg forever. He bade adieu to those ancient towers and dark forests; and issued forth beyond those walls behind which neither the excommunications of Leo X. nor the sword of Carles V. were able to restrain him."

As Luther went to Worms so he returned to Wittemberg, determined to enter though there were in it as many devils as there were tiles upon the housetops! He entered! and soon the announcement, "Luther is come!" "Luther is come!" flew through the place like flashes of lightning, and were felt like the electric shock. All at once, too, all the Anabaptist prophets were missing, Cellarius only excepted. Eight sermons from Luther produced wonderful effects. "At the command of Luther," says D'Aubigne, p. 596, "objections vanished, tumult was appeased, sedition ceased to vociferate her clamor, and the citizens of Wittemberg resumed the tranquil occupations of life."...."Nevertheless, Stubner, having been informed that the sheep of his flock had dispersed, returned speedily to his old haunts. Those who had remained constant to '*the celestial prediction*,' surrounded their master, recounted to him the substance of Luther's discourses, and impatiently inquired of him what course they ought in consequence to pursue."

Stubner and Cellarius were, or pretended to be, confident that they could defend their claims before Luther, and demanded an interview. Their request was granted, and the result was as might be expected. The following is a brief sketch of the conference, as recorded by D'Aubigne on p. 597. "Stubner was allowed to speak first. He explained how he wished to renew the Church and to change the world. Luther listened to this harangue with great calmness. At last, with great gravity, he replied. 'Nothing of what you have said is founded upon the Holy Scriptures, all your affirmations are made up of fables.' When these words were uttered, Cellarius was unable longer to restrain his fury. He commenced to speak; he made violent gestures; stamped with his feet, and struck with his hand the table that stood before him.

He worked himself into a passion, and exclaimed it was shameful to dare in this manner to speak to a man of God. Then Luther quietly added, 'St. Paul declares that the proofs of his apostleship have appeared through the working of wonders, prove yours by the performance of miracles. 'We will do so,' responded the prophets. 'The God I adore,' said Luther, 'shall well know how to hold your gods in check.' Stubner, who had preserved a larger portion of self-possession, fixing at this moment his eyes upon the Reformer, said, with the air of one inspired, 'Martin Luther, I am about to declare to you the thoughts which are now passing in your soul!.... you begin to believe that my doctrine is true.' Luther, having for a few moments remained silent, replied, 'God reprove thee, Satan.'....At these words all the prophets became furious. 'The Spirit, the Spirit!' they bellowed out. Luther, adopting, with a cold tone of disdain, the cutting familiar language peculiar to himself, said, 'I have hit your Spirit on the snout.' The clamor now increased two-fold, and Cellarius especially distinguished himself by his ravings. He became frantic, he shook and foamed at the mouth. No one could at this time be heard in the chamber of the conference. At last the three prophets abandoned the place, and on the same day quitted the city of Wittemberg." Thus it was that the novelties of the fanatical Anabaptists were met by the great Reformer, and thus it was that the new prophets were routed, at least for the present. But though they have fled from Wittemberg they have not abandoned their errors or ceased to propagate them. We must, therefore, follow them a little further.

On p. 741, our historian gives us the following account of their further proceedings:

"The fanaticism of the Anabaptists, extinguished in Germany at the time of Luther's return to Wittemberg, reappeared with increased strength in Switzerland, and it threatened to overthrow the edifice which Zwingle, Haller, and Ecolampade had reared upon the foundation of the word of God. Thomas Munzer, when forced to leave Saxony in the year 1521, had retreated to the very frontiers of Switzerland. Conrad Grebel, whose restless and ardent disposition we have already had occasion to describe, was bound in ties of amity with Munzer as well as Felix Mantz, the son of a canon, and some other citizens of the town of Zurich; while Grebel had likewise endeavored to gain the support of Zwingle. In vain had this Swiss reformer advanced in that direction further than Luther; for he now beheld a party eager to outstrip the progress he had made. 'Let us form,' said Grebel to Zwingle, 'a company of true believers; because it is to them alone the promise belongs; and let us establish a Church wherein sin shall not be allowed to enter.' 'It is impossible,' replied Zwingle, 'to form a heaven upon earth; and Christ has taught us that we must allow the tares to grow along with the wheat.' Grebel, being frustrated in his attempts with the reformer, longed to make an appeal to the people. 'The whole community of Zurich,' said he, 'must, with sovereign power, decide upon the affairs of faith.' But Zwingle feared the influence these radical enthusiasts might exercise upon the minds of a numerous assembly."

Three things should be noticed, just here, in the doings of these fanatics. First, while by proselyting and in other ways they are endeavoring to tear the church to pieces, they nevertheless cry out loudly for union! Second, they at the same time declare that the church is all wrong they only are right, and are going to have a church "wherein sin shall not be allowed to enter." Third, they flatter the people, cry out for their rights, and declare that "the whole community must with sovereign power decide upon the affairs of faith." We too have seen this game played: union has been loudly called for, while at the same time the work of proselyting has been carried on, and our Church represented as no church, and our baptism as no baptism; and, as of old, the people have been appealed to and flattered! But this game did not succeed with Luther and Zwingle; the German and Swiss reformers were not to be taken in this way; for though the "Swiss reformer advanced in that direction further than Luther," he soon discovered his mistake, and it was well he did, for the character and designs of the Anabaptist prophets soon became painfully apparent, as the following extracts from the same history will show.

"Repulsed by Zwingle, Grebel turned his attention elsewhere. Rubli, the ancient pastor of Basil, Brodtlein, the pastor of Zollekon, and likewise Herzer, received his advances with eagerness. They resolved to form an independent community in the centre of the grand community, a church in the middle of the church. A NEW BAPTISM was fixed upon as the means of gathering together their congregation, composed exclusively of true believers. 'The baptism of infants,' said they, 'is a horrible abomination, a manifest impiety, invented by the evil spirit and Nicholas II. the pope of Rome.' The council of Zurich, alarmed at the prospect of these proceedings,

issued an order for the observance of a public discussion; and the Anabaptists, still refusing to forsake their errors, some people of Zurich belonging to their sect were cast into prison, while a few strangers were banished from the district. But this persecution only served to augment the fervor of these enthusiasts." . . . . "Some of their number, begirt with cords or willow wands, walked through the streets, exclaiming, 'in a few days Zurich shall be destroyed. Wo to you, Zurich! wo, wo!' Many of them gave vent to expressions of blasphemy. 'Baptism,' said they, 'is the bathing of a dog, there is no more use in baptizing an infant than in baptizing a cat.' Simple people were thrown into a state of commotion and dread. Fourteen men, and among their number Felix Mantz, in company with seven women, were taken into custody, in spite of the intercession of Zwingle, and condemned to live upon bread and water in the tower of the heretics. At the end of fifteen days' confinement, they succeeded in raising some planks during the night, and, with the assistance of each other, they effected their escape. 'An angel,' they said, 'had opened the prison and procured their deliverance.' A monk who had fled from his convent, George Jacobade Coire, surnamed Blaurock, because he always wore, as it would appear, a blue habit, joined the newly-formed sect, and was, on account of his natural eloquence, denominated the second St. Paul. This bold Monk went about from place to place, obliging people to receive the token of his baptism by means of his overheated appeals. On a certain Sunday, in Zollekon, at the moment when the deacon was delivering his sermon, the impetuous Anabaptist interrupted the speaker by exclaiming in a voice of thunder, 'It is written my house is a

house of prayer, but ye have made it a den of thieves,' then, raising a stick he carried in his hand, he struck with it on the ground four violent blows, exclaiming, 'I am the door, he who will enter through me shall find food. I am the good shepherd. My body I give up to prison; my life I give up to the sword, to the funeral pile, or to the wheel. I am the commencement of baptism and of the bread of the Lord.'"

"But Zwingle offering a stern opposition to the torrent of Anabaptism in Zurich, St. Gaul was very soon overrun with the same plague. Grebel arrived in the latter city, where he was received with acclamations by his brethren; and on Palm Sunday, proceeding in company with an immense number of his adherents to the banks of the Sitter, he administered baptism to the whole multitude.

"After this, the spirit of fanaticism displayed itsel in freaks of melancholy extravagance. Pretending that our Lord exhorts us to become like little children, these unhappy beings began to jump about in the streets, and to clap their hands together, to dance round and round in numerous circles, to sit down upon the ground, and to roll one another about in the sand. Some of them threw the New Testament into the fire, saying: 'The letter kills, but the Spirit gives life;' while many, falling into convulsions, pretended they had received revelations of the Spirit."

But the most melancholy of all that D'Aubigne records concerning the Anabaptists, is that which he records just here, p. 744: "In a lonely house situated in the vicinity of St. Gaul, upon the Müllegg, there lived an old husbandman, eighty years of age, named John

Shucker, who had five sons to bear him company. The whole of this family, as well as their servants, received the ordinance of the new baptism, and two of the sons, Thomas and Leonard, particularly distinguished themselves by their extreme fanaticism. On the 6th February, 1526, the day being Shrove Tuesday, they invited a large number of Anabaptists to meet in their house, and the father killed a calf to provide for the feast. The viands and the wine sufficed to heat the imaginations of this numerous company, and they passed the whole night in conversation, fantastic gesticulations, convulsions, visions, and revelations.

"In the morning, Thomas, still excited by the excesses of the past night, and having even, as it would appear, lost the power of his reason, took up the bladder of the calf and put into it the gall of the beast, desiring thus to imitate the symbolical actions of the prophets; and, going up to his brother Leonard, he said to him in a sombre tone, 'Equally bitter is the death which you must die.' Then added, 'Brother Leonard, kneel down upon your knees.' Leonard did as he was commanded. In a little while he said, 'Brother Leonard, arise;' and Leonard again stood upon his feet. The father, the brothers, and the rest of the Anabaptists, stared in amazement, wondering what might be the will of God. Very soon Thomas once more said, 'Leonard, kneel down again,' and the humble posture was resumed. The spectators, alarmed at the gloomy expression of the unhappy actor, said, 'Reflect upon what you are about to do, and take care that no evil happens.' 'Do not fear,' replied Thomas, 'the will of the Father alone shall be fulfilled.' . . . . At the same moment he hastily seized a sword and aiming a blow with all his strength at the body of his kneeling brother, like a criminal before the executioner, he cut off his head, and exclaimed, 'Now the will of the Father is accomplished.' . . . . On the 16th of February, the wretched fratricide was beheaded by the hands of the hangman, and fanaticism had been seen to expend its last effort. The eyes of all were opened; and, as an ancient historian has said, 'the same blow served to decapitate alike the body of Thomas Shucker and that of Anabaptism in St. Gaul.' The sect, however, still lived in Zurich; and on the 6th of November of the preceding year, a public dispute had there taken place, in order to give satisfaction to the Anabaptists, who continued to cry out, 'The innocent are condemned without being heard.' The three following theses were proposed by Zwingle and his friends as the subject of conference, and were victoriously maintained by them in the hall of the Council." Here follow the theses:

"Children born of faithful parents are the children of God, like those who were born under the Old Testament; and, consequently, they can receive baptism."

"Baptism is, under the New Testament, that which circumcision was under the Old, consequently baptism must so now be administered to children in the same way as circumcision was formerly administered."

"The usage of baptizing anew cannot be proved, either by example, or by passages, or by arguments drawn from the Scriptures; and those who submit to a new baptism crucify Jesus Christ."

Here is a faithful account of the origin of the people called Anabaptists, and of some of their opinions and doings. John Matthias, the baker, and John Boccold, the tailor, have already been referred to as leaders of the Anabaptists; they too, claimed to be prophets, and Boccold finally proclaimed himself king by Divine appointment, and his fanatical followers obeyed him as such. They took possession of Munster, an imperial city of Westphalia. I think it was here that Matthias was killed.

It will be seen from the historic records here given, that these Anabaptists did not even claim to have obtained their teachings from the Bible; indeed they commenced by rejecting the Bible, as may be seen by reference to the above quotations; some of them actually threw their Bible into the fire. They claimed to have received their teachings by direct revelation; they said "We hold familiar conversation with the Lord." Some said they had a communication from the Angel Gabriel. Another, a little more honest, said, "I am the commencement of baptism," meaning, of course, baptism as he taught and practised. It will be seen, too, that Melancthon called their Antipedobaptist doctrine a "new doctrine." Nor does it appear that the prophets themselves denied this. As for Luther, when he heard the prophets state their own views, he said, and said truly, "All your affirmations are made up of fables!" It is also worthy of remark, that in the "Theses" quoted above, the reformers take the ground that "Baptism is under the New Testament that which circumcision was under the Old." And with regard to *re-baptizing*, they not only affirm that it has absolutely no countenance from the word of God, but they look upon the act as involving very serious consequences; and they not only censured the *re-baptizers*, but they went as far as to say that

"Those who submit to a new baptism crucify Jesus Christ!"

Such were the *men* who introduced the Antipedobaptist novelty; such the *time* and *mode* of its introduction: and such the *opposition* that it met with *from the great reformers of the sixteenth century.* "But it does not appear, " says Bishop Tomlin, " that there was any congregation of Anabaptists in England till the year 1640." And with regard to their commencement in this country, we are informed that it was on this wise. In Rhode Island, Ezekiel Holliman baptized Roger Williams, then Roger turned round and baptized Ezekiel and ten others. Such was their beginning in this western world. Such is the Church that claims to be the only Church, and such the baptism that is claimed to be the only baptism.

Now, we have no sympathy with what is called " the doctrine of succession," no sympathy with the cry, " We have Abraham to our father;" if people are wrong *now*, we censure them, whoever their father may have been; and if they are right now, we ask no more. But when the Anabaptists vainly, and loudly, talk about their antiquity and ancestry, and claim to be the Church, the only Church, and represent all others as having gone out of the way, it is highly proper, we think, to say to them, "Look to the rock whence ye are hewn, and to the hole of the pit whence ye are digged." So far as the Anabaptists are right *now* we are with them, and bid them God speed; but they must not expect us to indorse the inventions of Munzer, Grebel, Storck, Stubner, Boccold, and other fanatics, as being the teachings of Jesus and his Apostles. So far as they hold the truth in common with evangelical Christians, we are with them, and give them due credit, but when they reject what we know to be of Divine appointment, and force upon us what we know to be an unscriptural novelty, we may not submit, nor hold our peace either! And when they are so bigoted and exclusive that they will not sit down with God's people at God's table, or allow any of God's people to sit down with them at their table, let them not cry out for union Only a few days since, I was told the following: A lady who was a member of the M. E. Church, feeling that she was dying, sent for her pastor to administer to her the sacrament of the supper, feeling, like her Master, that she should not again drink of this fruit of the vine until that day when she should drink it new in her father's kingdom. The minister hastens to the dying room, the table is spread, and a little group of friends gather around to partake, with the dying woman, of the sacred emblems of Christ's dying love. The husband of the dying woman is in the next room; he is invited to come and receive the holy sacrament with his wife before she dies; but no, he will not: Why? Simply because he belongs to the Baptist Church, and his wife belongs to the M. E. Church! As we said before, so we say again, when such people cry out for union, which they do, under given circumstances, we must doubt their sincerity, we cannot do otherwise! And we verily believe that, till they are ashamed of, and abandon this unchristian practice, they should be left to themselves! And let it be remembered, that their claims to superiority are based upon the novelties that they received from the German fanatics of the sixteenth century! Once more, let them take the Gospel, which they hold, and preach it to sinners, and save all they can, and we will, so far bid them God speed. But let them not come into our churches and dwellings to pervert and proselyte those whom God has placed under our care, and who, *we know*, have received Scripture baptism! Let them not do this thing!

And now, ye people of Israel, Christian people of every name, we say to you in conclusion, Consecrate your children to God in holy Baptism; remember "the promise is to you and to your children;" and Jesus says to you, "Suffer little children to come unto me, and forbid them not, for of such is the kingdom of God." Bring, then, your children to Jesus, who is as ready now, and as able, to *bless them*, as He was when He first uttered those blessed words. Bring them, I say, to this blessed Saviour, who in the days of His flesh "took the little children up into His arms, put His hands upon them and blessed them." He claims them as the purchase of His blood, and "the free gift" has already "come upon" them "unto justification of life." Bring them, I say once more, to Him who died for them, and who commands you to do so; and as you come, say:

"We bring them, Lord, in thankful hands,
And yield them up to Thee,
Joyful that we ourselves are Thine,
Thine let our offspring be."

And when you baptize "with water," see that you baptize as He does, who baptizes "with the Holy Ghost;" and you *know* he baptizes by POURING, SHEDDING, FALLING; not by plunging!

www.ingramcontent.com/pod-product-compliance
Lightning Source LLC
LaVergne TN
LVHW021406110826
845150LV00007B/1809

9781425511807